LOOKING BACK

LOOKING BACK

THIRTY-TWO PEOPLE FACING DEATH
TEACH US HOW TO LIVE

MICHAEL SHIMA

WYETH HALL PRESS
NEW YORK, NEW YORK

Published by:
Wyeth Hall Press
P.O. Box 86
Planetarium Station
New York, New York 10024-0086
(800) 652-1954

Copyright © 1996 by Peter Shimamoto.
First Printing 1996.
Printed and bound in the United States of America.

Library of Congress Catalog Card Number: 95-90563.

ISBN 0-9646749-2-0

This book is dedicated to my parents.

ACKNOWLEDGMENTS

I would like to thank the hospices that helped me find the people I interviewed for this book. The individuals with whom I had direct contact at the hospices were Shelby Anderson, Susan Andres, Ginger Cave, Kit Cosgrove, Connie Dahlin, Douglas Gibson, Mary Halsey, Claire Hebert, Cheryl Henry, Gwen Heyman, Myra Kazanjian, Sheree Myer, Ann Reddy, Tracy Schroen, Donna Skurzak, Roberta Reynolds Spencer, and Lonnie West. There were other individuals who also provided assistance, but whose names I do not know, and I would like to thank them as well. I am particularly grateful to Mary Cooke of Cabrini Hospice, for without her help, I might never have gotten started.

Many thanks also to Judith Appelbaum and Florence Janovic of Sensible Solutions, whose advice and counsel were invaluable, and to Robert Nassau for his assistance and encouragement, as well as his patience in listening to me obsess about this project.

Finally, I would like to thank the people who allowed me to interview them for this book, and who were so gracious in sharing their time—and their lives—with me.

CONTENTS

INTRODUCTION

How should I live my life?

It is a question most of us probably do not ask ourselves often enough. Although we all know that eventually we are going to die, we generally manage to keep this certainty of our ultimate demise buried deep in the farthest corners of our minds. Accordingly, instead of appreciating each day to the fullest, we plod through our daily routines—getting up, going to work, going to the store, cooking dinner, paying the bills. We take our lives for granted, assume we still have plenty of time left, and put off until "later" the things we truly want to do, or know we should do.

Usually, it is only when something particularly unpleasant occurs—an especially bad day at work, an argument with a spouse or friend, the illness or death of a loved one—that we step back and examine the directions our lives have taken. Then we wonder if we are spending too much time at work and not enough with our family and friends; if we have become too concerned with acquiring "more" (money, power, possessions, etc.), rather than appreciating what we have; if we have fallen into a rut from which we can no longer extricate ourselves—if we are letting our lives pass us by.

This book consists of thoughts and reflections about life by people with terminal or serious illnesses. The premise behind the book is that men and women who have had to face the very real possibility that they may be nearing the end of their lives may understand more clearly than the rest of us what is truly important. What made them happiest? What gave their lives the most meaning? What, if anything, do they wish they had done differently? What advice do they have for others?

I decided to write this book because I was working in a job that I did not enjoy, but which paid me what many people might consider a substantial salary. Although I appreciated the money, I suspected that, if I continued to work in a job that was unfulfilling, I would ultimately regret it. I therefore thought it would be helpful to talk to people who were approaching the end of their lives and ask them what they considered most important.

In searching for people to interview, I decided to focus on hospice patients. I chose hospice patients because most hospices accept only people who have been diagnosed as having terminal illnesses and are expected to live for a limited period (usually less than six months). For most hospice patients, then, death is not some abstract event that will occur in a comfortably distant future, but a stark and imminent reality. This book explores how people view life when they know that the remainder of their own lives can be measured in some finite period—months, weeks, or even days; when they know that, for them, there is not much time left.

The interviews in this book were conducted in 1993 and 1994. They encompass a broad cross-section of Americans, as the interviewees lived in fourteen cities from coast to coast and ranged in age from their thirties to their eighties. They include, among others, a Catholic nun, a woman who suffered from agoraphobia, people who lived through the Depression, a man who fought in World War II, a man who fought in Vietnam, a person who was adopted and located his birth mother when he was in his forties, a man who adopted his neighbor's baby when the mother passed away a few weeks after giving birth, people who grew up in large families and those who grew up in small ones, people who live in the city and those who live in the country, grandmothers and grandfathers, people who are straight and those who are gay. Therefore, in addition to providing guidance as to what is most important in life, these interviews also constitute a useful record of what it is like to live in the United States in the twentieth century.

The book is organized according to certain themes that appear in the interviews, such as the importance of family, friends, or religion. This structure is highly subjective, as all the interviews cover many different subjects; however, I have arranged the interviews in the manner I felt was most appropriate.

Working on this book has been a valuable experience for me. Almost without exception, the interviewees seemed to be truly wonderful people, and I learned a great deal from them. I hope others will find the interviews useful as well. At the very least, they should remind us that life is a marvelous, but fleeting, gift, and that we should do our utmost to appreciate it while we can.

1

Family

When asked what had given them the greatest happiness, many of the interviewees replied, "Family." For these people, family provided what may well be the most important things in life: someone to care about them, and about whom they could care—someone with whom they could share their lives.

PATRICIA HUNT
CABRINI HOSPICE

I was born in Bronx, New York, raised in Brooklyn. I was born August 23, 1961. I'm thirty-two years old. I have three children. I've been married twelve years. I have a very good marriage. My husband and I get along very well, which is a rarity these days. We all get along fine.

I'm basically into family. I don't work. I chose to stay home, rather than go out and work, because I feel my children would benefit more from me being at home with them, rather than me going out to work. . . . I didn't want latchkey children.

My husband works. It's a traditional family—the mother stays home and takes care of the children, and the father goes out to work. That's basically how we live.

My son is eleven, I have a daughter that's eight and another daughter that's three. I didn't want them too close together, but then I didn't want them too spaced apart either. I wanted them whereas I can have time with all three of them. Which I did. And I was the type of mom where we did everything together. Family thing all the way. We went to pools together, we went to the beach together—we did everything basically together.

. . .

I decided that I wanted to have a family that did things together. I wanted what I call a "normal" family. I wanted my husband and I to get along. I wanted my children to get along. I wanted us all to get along. To me, that's happiness.

There's nothing better to me. You can have all the money—big time job, big time cars, whatever. That doesn't

3

make you happy. It's happiness when my husband comes, and brings the kids to visit me. And we're sitting here, and we're laughing and we play together. That's happiness, to me. Going outside and eating Kentucky Fried Chicken and all that—that's not happiness. At the time, it's fun. It's not happiness to me. Happiness to me is when we go to the beach, and I watch them go run in the water, and a wave chases them. My husband and I, we laugh at that. That's funny. We watch my three year old chasing a wave, and the wave's chasing her. Or when we're at the movies, and we're all trying to be quiet, and somebody drops the soda, and we're all [makes sound of muffled laughter]. That's fun. That's life. We're actually living. That's happiness to me.

When my children get awards in school—that's happiness. We were at my son's graduation this past June, and he got an award from the Comptroller for being one of the top students in school. That's happiness. Because my husband and I were there. That's happiness. Because, out of the audience, there were maybe five or six men participating in their sons' graduation. That's happiness because my husband, my son, my daughters were there. And to look around in the audience and see only four or five men . . . . To me that shouldn't be. There should be more men in the audience participating in their sons' graduation. To me, that's happiness, because to me, that's a true traditional family setting.

. . .

When I was growing up, I didn't really think about family. When I was growing up, actually, I wanted to be a career woman. . . . I wasn't thinking about marriage. I wanted to live big time. . . . I was thinking about getting a job. I wanted a nice, big old house, a car. That's what I thought I wanted at that time in my life. I wasn't thinking about no man; that's the last thing I wanted. I was like, "What can a man do for me?" He can't do anything for me that I can't do for myself. Children? Ha! That was the last thing on my mind, was a kid. No way. I would have to be like, twenty-five or thirty before I even thought about kids. This is when I was growing up. This is how I thought at the time.

At that time, I thought, "A kid? No way." I thought I would be barefoot and pregnant, with some man telling me what to do. I thought, "No, that's not for me." That's not what I wanted. That was not on my menu at that time.

So what happened to change things?

I grew up. I grew up. When I was about seventeen or eighteen, I grew up. When I became pregnant at nineteen, that's what changed everything. At that time, I didn't want an abortion, but yet, I didn't want to get on welfare. I didn't want to be part of what they call "the system." Young black girl from a broken home . . . being pregnant at nineteen, at that time, that was kind of good, because I wasn't fifteen. Even today, even ten years ago, it was like, the usual. Young black girl from a broken family, being pregnant, getting on welfare, nobody to help her with her child, just her and her child. The boyfriend is still there living with her, or she's living with her mother. Even if her and the boy do get an apartment together, he's there, but she's not telling the system that. . . . They're doing drugs. She keeps having babies. And he's just there, no job. Hanging out with his friends, drinking beer, doing drugs.

What made me change was, I didn't want that. I didn't want to be caught in the system, like everybody else. At the time, Stephen and I weren't married. But he felt pretty much the same way I felt. We didn't want to have a child we couldn't take care of. He wasn't into abortion. And we were like, "What are we going to do?" We had to change. We couldn't just have this child, and I go on welfare, and him still living here. We had to do something.

He wasn't working. I said, "I don't care what kind of job

5

you get, as long as you get a job." And he was like, "Okay, I'll get a job."

We didn't want to be like other people—I'm on welfare, and he's living off of me. The so-called "norm" for young black people at that time. Stephen and I didn't want to be like those other people. We wanted to change things, and make things better for us and this unborn child I was carrying.

I did get pregnant out of wedlock. I was partly ashamed, and partly not. I wanted a child, but I felt kind of ashamed having a child out of wedlock—that was my personal hang-up at that time. I did manage to finish high school. That was one thing . . . well, not one thing . . . I've accomplished a lot of things in life, as far as I'm concerned. I did get out of high school, that was a good thing. Stephen did get his GED. So we were a little different from other people. . . . Stephen got a job as a photo technician. . . . He's been there now, twelve years.

We got an apartment in the Bedford-Stuyvesant area of Brooklyn. We still live there now. Everybody in the neighborhood knows us now, and we know everybody in the neighborhood now. We are part of the neighborhood. Stephen's been working there for the last twelve years, and he's doing real great. I became a PTA mom. I volunteered in the school. My son just graduated from the neighborhood school. He was one of the top students there. My daughter is going into the fourth grade, and she's going into the top fourth grade class. My son was just in the gifted program, and he's continuing in the gifted program. He goes to the junior high school now in the neighborhood. He's in the second highest program.

. . .

[During a break in the interview, Ms. Hunt was told, for the first time, that her illness was terminal, and that the doctors didn't know how long she would live; they said it could be two days, or two years.]

. . .

Do you think there's any particular meaning or purpose to life?

I think we're all put here for some reason or another, and I think my reason was to help people and show people that the true meaning of life is happiness. Without happiness, you can never truly enjoy life. To enjoy life, you have to be able to enjoy the people around you—your children, your husband or wife—because they are the most important people in the world. And without someone to help you share, you can never truly be happy. Everybody needs somebody. . . . All of us need somebody to talk to, or to be with. All of us.

When you leave from talking with me, or your day's ended, you're going to need your girlfriend, or your friend. You're going to need an outlet. You're going to need that person. You're going to say, "I spoke to her, and she's just finding out today that she had only two days, or two years to live; she didn't know that she only had that little bit of time to live." . . . Like I said, you need to go home and speak to the persons close to you, and be able to tell them things like that. To me, that's part of happiness—that's part of life. We all need that. That's my message to you, and to other people. That's what my purpose in life is—to tell people that all of us need somebody. You're going to go home, and you're going to need to tell somebody—"She doesn't know whether she's going to live today or tomorrow."

Is there anything you wish you'd done differently?

That's a hard one. . . . That's a hard question. . . .

Is there anything that you wanted to do . . . ?

Oh, there's a lot of things I wanted to do. There's just so much life has to offer. Life has a lot to offer. I'm not going to say, "Oh, I wish that this was different." Some things are not meant to be. If it had been meant for me to go to college and be a brain surgeon, then I would have gone to college to be a brain surgeon. . . . But I don't think I would have been happier if I'd done that. Because if I had gone to college and been a brain surgeon, I wouldn't have been part of this family.

Do you have any advice for other people?

Well, I don't really like to tell other people what to do with their life. It's their life, and the decisions they make in life are their own. And they have to make the best decisions, and handle it. Whatever decisions they make in life, they should be able to handle it.

. . .

My children are young—eleven, eight and three. I would like them to know that their mother did think about them. And I loved my children. My children were my life. I know I loved my children dearly. . . . I'll tell anybody and everybody that I'm conceited; yes, I am. I think my children are the best children in the world; I feel that I'm the best mom in the world. That's how I feel—that I'm the best and they are the best. And no one, I feel, is better than us. My husband, I feel, is a brilliant man.

. . .

I want my kids to know that I did love them . . . and to let them know their mom only lived these couple of years, but in the years that they did know me, that I did do a lot to help them. Because I did. As far as teaching them how to swim, watching them run away from the waves, and one time we had a snowball fight, and one time in the fall we watched the foliage, watching the apples grow. . . . I do want them to know that this is dedicated to them. . . . They used to get angry that I used to make them do their school work, but it paid off. My son's in the gifted program, and my daughter is in the top class

8

in her school as well. . . . I think that I did a whole lot for them, and it paid off. It was tough, but to me, it paid off.

And I want them to know that I dedicate my whole life to them, because they were, and are, indeed, my life.

❧

NORA WELSH
ANGELA HOSPICE

I was born in Canada, in 1910. I'm eighty-three years old. I came from a family of twelve—eight girls and four boys, still ten of us living. I'm the second oldest.

We've been here [near Detroit, Michigan] since 1927. I have two sisters living in Florida—they're nuns. I have five sisters who are nuns.

Did you ever think of becoming a nun yourself?

Oh no, no way. Not for me. The oldest girls got married. And then the next five went in the convent. One brother died when he was twelve—he was drowned, in Canada, the year before we came here.

. . .

I got married when I was twenty-one. I met my husband in the restaurant where I was working. He worked for the Wabash Railroad at the time. . . . We went four years before we got married. I was married in 1931.

I don't have any children. I have no family—just my brothers and sisters. My husband died twenty-two years ago, so I've been alone, on my own.

. . .

I like Michigan. It's got all the different climates, which is good. It's good to get away too. I've seen a lot of country. My husband and I did a lot of traveling after he retired. I've been to Ireland, and I've been to Hawaii, and I've been in every state but Alaska, I guess. We've done a lot of traveling. My husband's niece and her husband—the four of us—used to take a lot of trips. I like to travel. I love to go. I like people.

I just came back from Florida. I was there for two weeks at my sisters'. They told me I should get out and go, so I did. I enjoyed it. I really got a lot of good rest.

. . .

We have a reunion up in Canada every three years. In fact, I was up there in August for a reunion on my dad's side—the first one they've ever had. And they had about five or six hundred people there. For three days, we really had a great time.

On my mom's side, we have it every three years. So we go out to the old homestead—the farm—and they have it out there. We've been going there for the last fifteen, twenty years probably.

. . .

Did you enjoy living in Canada?

When I lived there, it was different. I wouldn't go back and live there now. It's a small town. Mom said we'd all have to go away from home, and she didn't go for that, to get a job or something, because it was just a small little country town— farm country mostly. I did enjoy it, because we had an uncle with a farm up on the lake, and we'd go up there picking berries—wild berries, not the tame ones like they have now. We had to wash by hand, and bake our bread by letting it sit overnight, and all that. It was a lot different than it is today. People don't believe what we went through.

We enjoyed it. We had a good time. We did a lot of square dancing. Our place was quite the place for people to come. They were always coming. Mom and dad would be in bed, and they'd come, wanting to have a square dance. And mom would get up and let them in.

. . .

We moved to Michigan because of work. To keep the family together, is what mom wanted. She didn't want us to be all over the country. Which I can see—you have to go where you get the work. . . . I didn't seem to mind moving. . . . I think I was kind of glad to get away from the small town—they know everything that's going on.

. . .

Is there anything in particular that's made you the happiest?

Just having good friends, and making friends with people. I belong to a lot of senior clubs. Not as many as I did. But right now, I go to our old one, that I belonged to for thirty-six years. I go back there—I don't live in the neighborhood anymore—but I go back there every Wednesday.

I love sports. I love baseball. Any kind of sports.

. . .

Are there any times in your life that stand out as being especially memorable?

I never gave that a thought. So many things have happened—good things and bad things.

. . .

I worked at Hudson's for thirty-one years. Hudson's was like Marshall Field's and Macy's department store. . . . I had a

11

lot of friends down there. I still have—they call me from New York and all over, wherever they're at. I got to know a lot of people. We used to have picnics. I've done a lot of cooking for them. They had me do the cooking. They said, "You do the cooking—we'll come and get you." [Laughs.]

. . .

I kept busy. I like to do things. I don't like to be sitting around. I used to have around fifty people on New Year's Day for dinner. I had friends, and mostly nieces and nephews, and brothers and sisters. I've got a lot of nieces and nephews, and great-nieces and great-nephews. I couldn't tell you how many—there's a slew of them.

They've been very good to me too—they call me. Since I've been sick, they just . . . . And then I've got one of my sisters living with me. She's a nun. She's been with me since December 14. They don't want me to be alone.

And the people at hospice are just marvelous. I've never seen anything like them.

. . .

I have cancer. I first learned about it in December. My leg was swelling up, and it just got so it felt like it was going to burst. So my brother came and took me to the doctor, and she put me in the hospital right away. She said, "You got a blood clot." I said, "Can I go home?" And she said, "No way. You're going right into the hospital." So I was in there for ten days, right on my back, with intravenous of all kinds. Then they took chest [x-rays] and they found the cancer.

How did you feel when you first learned that you had cancer?

Well you know, I kind of had a feeling. . . . And I wouldn't be operated on—not at eighty-three years old. No way. So I just take it every day, a day at a time. I know I'm not young anymore.

. . .

Is there anything in your life that you wish you'd done differently?

I guess there's a lot of things that I should have done differently. [Laughs.] Like everybody else. But I don't know—I wouldn't want to go back. The way things are today is just terrible. I feel sorry for people who have youngsters coming up today—the environment that they're getting into.

Do you have any idea about what the reason might be for all the problems we're having?

Well, I think the Second World War brought a lot of it on. And then the kids went to Vietnam and got the dope over there. And mothers and dads are both working, and the kids are left alone to do what they want to do. They just got everything they wanted—they were making such big money, and now they want it. Here we were, we were brought up, and we had nothing. We were wearing one another's clothes. But today they have to have all this real expensive stuff. It's too bad. But you can't blame the kids. I think a lot of it was brought on by the war.

Do you have any advice for other people about how they should live their lives?

They should be considerate of people, which they're not. As long as they get what they want, they don't care.

. . .

We're a very close family. That's one thing about us, is we're very close. Everybody looks out for one another. That makes it nice, when you have a close family. I've seen so many families who never see their family. I think I'd die if I had to go through that.

It sounds like you have a pretty good family.

One of the best, I would say. One of the best.

❧

HANS DYERSON
FAMILY HOME HOSPICE

I was born in Wisconsin, just south of Madison. Now I live in Las Vegas, Nevada. I was born in 1914—I'll be eighty next month. I grew up in a musical background. My parents were both musical. We were a musical family all the way. There were five kids in the family. My brother and I were on the circuit when we were kids. . . . We sang with several glee clubs. We were very interested in band music. We traveled a lot, from one theater to another. It was like a vaudeville.

I was six at the time, and my brother was three and a half. We started at an early age. I entered some of these contests they had on the road—medicine contests. I won every time I entered. When I was going to junior high school, I was what they would call now a bobby-soxer. Every Friday we'd have a concert in the auditorium. I always sang, and in the front row, they'd cheer and scream. I stopped after a while, because my voice changed. It changes when you're a teenager.

So then I went to work in a restaurant. And I did sing in

the restaurant. They had a cocktail bar, and I sang in there. My brother joined me, and we were on the radio.

I was back there a year ago, and he and I were rehearsing—even at our age—the songs we sang when we were on the stage.

We traveled in an old Model-T Ford. This was in the 1920's—a long time ago. . . .

Then when I got older, I went into the food and beverage business. I had several bars and restaurants in California and Illinois.

Then I sold everything I had and went to work in hotels. I liked that because I like people. I met a lot of people—a lot of big stars. They were very nice.

. . .

I met my wife on a dance floor in Belvidere, Illinois. It was love at first sight, on both sides. She was out there on the floor dancing, and I thought, "Now that's the girl for me." And that was her.

We both fell in love at the same time. I was twenty-four when I got married. It was on her twenty-first birthday. We had a good marriage. We were married forty-nine years, six months and exactly three days to the hour. I kept track. But I didn't get my fiftieth anniversary.

. . .

My wife got very sick—I was married to her for over forty-nine years. She passed away in 1988.

Then I became sick with this cancer. They found it in 1991, and they operated on me. They said I wouldn't see 1992. But I fought—I really fought. I didn't give up. . . . When I got the verdict that I was going to die, I said I wasn't going to die.

. . .

I was bedridden for a year and a half. I couldn't move my legs. I couldn't raise them for anything. A therapist came out

15

and showed me how to do bed exercises. And I'd do them all hours of the day and all hours of the night. I'd wake up and start those exercises. And then I got a walker. So I started walking with that. Then I gave that up and got a cane, and I started walking with a cane. Now I don't walk with anything. I put 'em away and said, "Now you're not going to run my life." I'm a stubborn guy. I just don't give up.

· · ·

When I got sick, I knew there was something wrong. When I was taking care of my wife while she was sick, I had signs of bleeding. My wife saw it when she did the laundry. She said, "You better go to the doctor." I said, "Oh, I'll be all right. It's probably just a pimple." I said to her, "Well, who's going to take care of you if I go to the hospital?" I had nobody there. We were alone. She said, "Well, you still ought to go." Well, I didn't go, and this is what happened. They found cancer. If I'd had that operation earlier, I don't think I would have had it.

That's all right. I'm not trying to be any hero or anything. I told her it was my obligation.

· · ·

I have an adopted son. His mother lived right next to my mother-in-law. That was in 1952. My mother-in-law looked in the window because she hadn't seen her outside with the baby. It was only seventeen days old. She looked in there and saw him and his mother laying on the floor. So she called the law, and they came out, and the mother was dead. She'd been dead since childbirth. He hadn't had anything to eat or anything. So they turned him over to us, because my mother-in-law was staying with us. So we took care of him. But he was a ward of the state. And then when my mother-in-law passed away, we had to decide what to do. So I got hold of a lawyer. . . .

My son's forty-two years old now. He's been the best son that I could ever have. . . . He doesn't smoke, he doesn't drink, he doesn't do drugs. He's never even had a speeding ticket or even a parking ticket. He's a fine boy. . . .

He took care of me when I got sick. If it hadn't been for him, I wouldn't be here today.

. . .

In May of last year, I got the courage award from the American Cancer Society. And then I got a letter from our Governor, congratulating me on being so courageous.

I also go out to see people at the hospital, and talk to them. I have several I call on the telephone. I've never even seen them, but I talk to them. I say, "Don't give up, just fight like I did." That seems to help.

. . .

I don't want to be declared a hero, because I'm not. I just want to help. If you can't help other people . . . it's a poor enough world as it is right now.

. . .

What are the things that have made you the happiest?

Music. The music made me happy. We had a lot of rehearsals, and a lot of competitions. And we really came up out of the pile.

. . .

Do you think there's any particular meaning or purpose to life?

Oh, absolutely. Life is wonderful. Life is beautiful. But you have to look at it the right way. Now you take everything to heart—what's going on in Europe, all over the world. They're fighting over what? That's pathetic. Killing each other. It's a shame. It's really a shame. And look what they're doing in these automobiles, going by and shooting people. It's terrible. I think last weekend, we had fourteen that were killed. It's really a pity, I tell you.

Is there anything in your life that you wish you'd done differently?

Yeah, I wish I'd gone farther in my music. If I come back—because I think there's a hereafter—I want a big bunch of musicians. And I want to show 'em what music really is. It's beautiful, but they're ruining it. I'm not a long-nosed guy or anything like that, but some of this is noise, not music. I want to come back and have a big band. I hope the big band comes back one of these days. I probably won't see it.

. . .

Do you have any advice for other people about how they should live their lives?

Not how they should live their lives. But if they get sick the way I got sick—fight. Don't give up. How they lead their own lives, I can't tell them how to lead their lives. I lived mine the best way I could.

. . .

I was just watching this story on television about these people who were married eight days, and are going to get divorced. That's a real married life. That's terrible.

Do you have any idea about why people don't seem to stay married that long these days?

They don't talk things over. Everything should be fifty-fifty. My wife and I never had any problems. My wife got the sixty and I got the forty, because I gave it to her. Most of the time, she was right. And I acknowledged that—that she was right. Why argue? We got along swell. We had no problems. I wish other people would be as happy as we were.

Except when she got sick. She was so sick. She went through a lot of pain. It was a blessing that she left, but you hate to see 'em go. . . . You've got to keep going regardless. But there's not a day I don't have a tear in my eye. You don't have to be a woman to cry.

❧

DOROTHY KING
ANGELA HOSPICE

I'm sixty-five years old. I live in Northville, Michigan [near Detroit]. I was born in Canada. I came over to this country when I was married in 1948. I'm divorced. I've been divorced for about eight years, after thirty-six years of marriage. I have three children. They're thirty-eight, thirty-four and thirty.

I belong to a singles ministry. That's really saved me through my divorce, after all those years. It was very difficult for me. And I found this ministry, and it's very unique. It helps a lot of people. That's been my source of comfort, other than my family, through this after my divorce.

It's a nondenominational singles ministry. . . . It's for singles only. It doesn't matter how you're single—we've got a never-married group, we have a widows and widowers group, and then there's a divorced group. . . . That's been my source of comfort through my divorce. Now I haven't been as active, because I don't have quite the energy I had before.

. . .

19

I tried to have a reconciliation with my husband this last year, in the fall, and I couldn't do it. There was nothing left of the marriage as far as I'm concerned, after all that time. . . . So now my source of happiness . . . I find that I'm not happy unless I'm with my family or friends. I just got back from Florida. I was gone for two weeks. I was with my sister, and I'd just been there a couple weeks before, but I'd only stayed a week. And I just wasn't as happy as I would have been if I was home with my own. . . . I just felt too lonely after a while.

With me, if I'm around my family or my friends, I'm as happy as I guess I can possibly get. There's nothing else left at my stage. You don't need that much, other than friendship and love from your family.

I have two sons. My two oldest are sons. The youngest just got married this year. The other one's still single. My daughter just came back from Texas. She'd been there for ten years. She just got divorced, so what a mess. But I'm happy they're all around me. She's been here with me since June, so it makes it quite nice. It beats living by yourself. I don't like living by myself. I think it's mostly because I haven't done it much. My older son lived with me until two years ago.

. . .

I grew up in Essex, Ontario. It's just outside of Windsor. . . . I have a couple brothers and a sister still over there. I have one sister who lives here. I had another sister who lived a block from me, but she died ten years ago. I came from a large family— seven kids. Another sister died in Canada. . . . I met my husband over there, and then came over here to live. At first it was difficult. I just had a hard time leaving my family. But after a year, I got okay. . . . When my daughter got married, she moved straight to Texas. It's difficult, because you're used to your family around you, and then when you don't have them, you just can't run and visit them. We talked almost every day for ten years on the phone. . . . We tried to stop it, but we just couldn't make it. It was hard.

20

We've always been pretty close, which is great. I hear so many people have such a hard time getting along with their daughters or family. It seems to me you just have to get along. There's really no point in doing anything else. . . . Actually, with your children, you could be nagging at them constantly, I suppose. And I think that's what a lot of people do. And it is easy to do, because you want the best for them. And the way it looks to them, when you're nagging—they don't like it that much. They're adults—they want to do what they want to do. You learn that over time.

Do you think there's any particular secret for getting along with your kids?

Not really. I don't think so. I think you have to have a real close talk with them all the time. I notice people who say, "You can't say this. You don't let them know this, and if they ask you a question, you don't tell them the truth." I know someone who would say, "My kids don't ask questions the way yours do." And I'd say, "Yeah, because you never tell them the truth anyway." She'd tell them the stork came and brought this baby. And you can't lie to kids like that. They're through with asking you questions. . . . So it turns out they don't ask you anything, and by the time they're adults, they're not close to you at all. I would think that has something to do with it. I don't really know for sure, but it's got to be something like that. And then they'll be able to come to you with anything, no matter whether you like it or not. And in time, you get used to whatever they're going to say to you. . . .

I guess if I had to say it, I guess that having a good relationship with your children has to be having to be able to talk to them at any level, at any time, almost at any age. People used to say that to me way back, "Oh, how do you have such a nice relationship with your kids?" And I thought, "Well, I don't know." But I think it's mostly because you have to be able to talk to them. And I listen to them too. My daughter used to say, "I don't really want advice, mom. I just want you to listen to me." And that was good advice for me. I need to stand back and listen to them.

I don't think there's anything they can't talk to me about now. All of them. I used to think, once in a while with my daughter, "Well, do I really want to hear this?" Telling me something that happened on a date. I'd think, "Oh no." But then I thought, "Well, if that's what she has to tell me, I guess I'll listen."

. . .

What are the things that have made you the happiest in your life?

Well, all through my life, it's been being around children—being around my own, being around my nieces. Before I married and came here, I was real close to my oldest sister, and she had children.

And when I first got divorced, I danced all the time. I used to dance four or five nights a week—ballroom dancing. I learned ballroom dancing, and we used to go out dancing all the time. I liked it, but then I got sick of it. Some people do it forever, but I did it for about three years, and I just didn't want to do it anymore. I used to go out dancing so many times, you wouldn't believe it. . . . But I saw these people who didn't grow. They were in the same place that they were, people said, twenty years ago. Still doing the same old thing. I thought, "Is this going to be me? Am I going to be dancing around, not having any commitment?"

Some of the stuff, I don't know if it made me really happy doing. I did it anyway, just to be doing something. I think a lot of people do that—they go to bars, they go here, and they hang out. You see them everywhere. . . .

As old as I was, my sister used to think that was the way you had to be—go to bars, and you dance. I used to be so depressed, I'd cry all the way home. This was when I first got divorced. And she'd say to me, "You can't take that stuff seriously." And I know people who still do that, but I can't handle it. . . .

You do all kinds of things to try to make yourself happy, but I don't know that a lot of the stuff really makes you as happy as you're hoping it will.

. . .

I have cancer. According to my doctor, I only have two more months—not even two more months—to live. But I don't feel like I only have two more months. But I don't know how you're supposed to feel either. So I'm hoping that maybe I'm not that sick.

. . .

Do you think there's any particular meaning or purpose to life?

Yes. I believe that, if we don't do for other people, what are we here for? And it's not just to get up in the morning and look good, or go to a job and do it. Not unless it's helping other people. I really think that you have to be helping other people to make your life worth living. I think that's why we're here on earth—to help your fellow man. Wherever you see need, you should do it. . . . You can't be happy just getting up and going dancing every night. . . . That's not enough. That's okay once in a while, but it's not enough to do that. . . . I think that's the purpose in life. But I think that some people can overdo that too. Some people get so involved in that, they forget they have a family. There's got to be a happy medium.

Is there anything in your life that you wish you'd done differently?

I don't think so. . . . I wish maybe things had turned out a little differently. I had all those years of marriage. Maybe I could have been a little more . . . I think in some ways I might have done a little bit too much for my children, instead of my husband. A lot of people do make that mistake. Certain men can handle it better, I guess. I don't know why I've always been so much for my children. But maybe I needed to be a little more of a wife than a mother, maybe.

❧

VIVIAN KRUDWIG
HOSPICE SAN ANTONIO

I was born in McKinney, Texas. It's a suburb of Dallas. It's right out of Dallas—it's practically in Dallas. I came to San Antonio when I was about eight years old. I'm really not good on dates of things that have passed. I forget—I look forward to the future. I used to. I have no future now, so I don't know what I'm going to do. [Laughs.] But I used to always look at the future, and when it's gone, it's gone, and I don't worry about it. So I really am not good on past dates. But I would imagine I was about eight years old when we moved to San Antonio, and we've been here ever since.

My husband was in the service—World War II. And that's pretty much it.

. . .

I like living in Texas. Being born and raised here, I don't think you'd find many people that wouldn't. We do have kind of a big head, I think. But it's justifiable. [Laughs.]

You can do and see everything in Texas. You really can.

And they're very friendly people. The people are different, I think. I don't know whether that's good or bad. But you go to different places, and have people ask you, "Are you from Texas?" And you think, "Is it written all over me?" How they know, I don't know. I don't know how they think of us, but we like Texas.

. . .

I have one sister. She also lives in San Antonio.

My sister and I were the only two children, but we had grandparents who had lots of children, and there were always children around us. Family is very important. In fact, I guess a family is about the most important thing anybody could have. It certainly has proven so now, with my situation, because my two sons have just given me all the support and love that they possibly could. My daughter-in-law was a nurse, and she's given up her life right now to take over for me, and help me, and do the things I can't. I have a very sweet daughter-in-law that just became an ex-daughter-in-law, and she's just as sweet as can be. . . . I have seven grandchildren, and what could anybody ask for that is better than that? They really are great kids.

The nice thing about it is—as kids grow older, they pretty well outgrow you. And these kids still stop by and just visit with us, and just yak, because they don't live too far from us. They like to just come by and yak with us. It's nice to know that children still like to enjoy you when you can't give 'em that extra cookie or something.

Well, I'm doing all the talking—you're supposed to do the questioning. This is my big problem. What bothers me more with my lung cancer than anything else is that, after I talk for a while, I get pretty winded. So I do an awful lot of talking while I can, it seems like.

When you were growing up, did you have any kind of plans for what you'd do when you became an adult?

25

Yep. A mommy and have babies. And I did. That's all I was ever interested in—having a family.

. . .

I met my husband walking down Houston Street. Houston Street at that time was where all the kids ganged up. Everybody always drove up and down Houston Street before they got ready to go home, around 11:00 at night. They'd just wave at people and say their goodnights, and there were no problems at all.

I can't believe how cheap kids think life is now. Something has to be done somehow. I would work out a way somehow if I didn't have this, I guarantee you. Because it has to stop. These kids have to learn what a family is, and what love is.

. . .

What are the things that have made you the happiest in your life?

My kids, my grandkids. My whole family. We're together an awful lot. We are a very close family. I don't know anybody, anywhere that could be any closer to their family than the Krudwig family. My sons are sweet, my daughters-in-law are sweet, I get sweet notes, I get sweet cards, I have flowers in my house.

They say you don't miss a thing if you don't have it, and that's true. But boy, if you don't have it . . . . My family has supported me in every way. They go with me, they help me make decisions. They've told me that they would back me any way I went—that they would support me no matter what my decision was. And that makes me feel awfully good.

. . .

I work with a market research company—Roper. We're based in New York. I got involved in that because I wanted to work part-time, and I did. My mother had a heart attack, and I would sit around and go to the hospital every day and see her. Finally we had to put her in a nursing home. And I would sit there with my husband—he retired young—and twenty-four hours together is really not for me or anybody else. So I decided I would go to work half a day. I thoroughly enjoyed it. I work with great people. They are such nice people. . . .

I have not allowed the people to know that I'm ill. They are beginning now—all of them—to know something is going on. They like me and I like them. I'm not blowing my own whistle, but we all get along—we're friends. And why should they suffer longer than they have to, knowing it all the time? That's the reason I didn't tell them. I just didn't want them to deal with it as long as I've been dealing with it.

I don't work full-time now, but I do something every day. A lot of times I do quite a lot of work, and some days I just don't do hardly anything, depending on how I feel. I have good days and I have bad days.

. . .

I thoroughly enjoy my work. That's the only thing . . . I would not have worked when my children were little anyway, because I wanted to be home with them. But that is the only thing that I would have changed—I would have gone to work sooner.

. . .

Are there any particular times in your life that stand out?

No, not really. I'd just say I've had a great life. If you look back at it, God has had His hand on my shoulder all along. Just like this working—I had never thought about working. But the opportunity came along, and I think God knew that I was going to need this. My husband says, "Honey, you can get on the expressway quicker than anybody else." God gets me on the expressway. [Laughs.] . . .

So really, everything in my life—I just know my life has kind of been planned by God, and I've tried to live up to it.

. . .

I hope I don't do things that I'm not supposed to do. We all sin, but we all ask for forgiveness. I hope for forgiveness.

Do you think there's any particular meaning or pur-pose to life?

Yes, I think everybody was put here for a purpose, and some of us don't know what it is. I'm not sure what my pur-pose is. I feel right now that it's to have a good time and enjoy my family, because that's really what I have done.

. . .

When I first learned I had lung cancer, they told me I could have six months without chemo or two years, maybe, with chemo. Well, six months or two years at that point in your life sounds like a big difference, so I chose chemo. I chose chemo last summer. But it made me so sick that I chose to stop it. I would have one good day and bang, I would have a chemo treatment, and I was wiped out. Quality is very important to me. If I couldn't have quality of life, I didn't want life. And that's what I chose. . . . I stayed with chemo just long enough to lose all my hair and have it come back a completely differ-ent color.

. . .

My attitude towards life hasn't changed since I found out I had cancer. I sure don't like the fact that I have cancer at all. But I also know there's nothing I can do about it. And it's God's will. I feel He's been very good so far, because I really have not suffered as much as I would think a lot of people suffer. It's one of those things.

I sure don't like it. If I had my choice, I'd be happy to throw it out the window—as long as one of my family didn't catch it.

. . .

Do you have any advice for other people about how they should live their lives?

Well, I'll tell you what my daddy told me, and what I think my sister and I both grew up on: Don't worry. If you can do something, do it. If you can't do anything about it, forget it, it's gone. Don't look back. But don't worry. If you can fix it, get out there and work hard and fix it. But if you can't, just forget it and don't moan over it.

That's pretty well the way I grew up, and my sister grew up. And our kids are growing up the same way. And my little grandkid the other day, she was skating. And the girl fell down, and she said, "Woops! Have to get up and try again!" It didn't mean a thing to her that she fell. She wanted to be sure to get up and try again. So it's getting instilled in her too. And I think that's great.

2

Family:
Part II

Unfortunately, family can be the source not only of great happiness, but also of great pain. This principle is illustrated by the story of Joan Lehman. Ms. Lehman was abused by a family member when she was a child, and the abuse haunted her for the rest of her life. Among other things, Ms. Lehman's story serves as a stark reminder of the terrible consequences of child abuse, which can create searing scars that never heal.

Fittingly, however, family was not an entirely negative factor in Ms. Lehman's life for, although it was the cause of her greatest suffering, it was also the source of her greatest joy.

JOAN LEHMAN
HOSPICE OF ST. JOSEPH COUNTY, INC.

I grew up in Mishawaka [Indiana]. I was born in Mishawaka. I was born in 1935. I'm fifty-nine. I was a Catholic, born a Catholic. I went to Catholic grade school, and two years to Catholic high school.

I have one brother, but he's the age of my son—there was that much difference between us. He'd be about thirty-eight, so there's quite a difference between us. He lives in Missouri, and I haven't heard from him in years. My mother died young, and my father got remarried when he was little. My father and step-mother didn't have nothing to do with me for years.

I was twenty when my mother died. My mother and dad are both dead.

I was married twice. . . . I was seventeen when I got married the first time. I met my husband at Notre Dame—I worked there, and he worked there too. I had two children. Then I left. . . . I was having problems [with my first husband]. I had agoraphobia—that's where you can't leave your house. It started when I was eighteen or nineteen. It started after I had my first kid.

I'd get diarrhea, vomiting, my heart would beat fast. I'd feel like I was going to pass out. At one time it would be so bad, I couldn't even move. But it did get better through the years. I started going to a psychiatrist, and that's when [I had problems with my first husband]. So I left, and I met my second husband.

My first husband got the kids. . . . We went to court, but we couldn't get them. So he adopted one out, and the other one he kept. The one that was adopted is in Alabama, but the girl, I don't know where she's at.

. . .

My parents were alcoholics. I had a very rotten life. I was sexually molested when I was seven, by my grandfather. They claim that's what caused the agoraphobia. And I still have agoraphobia. But I can get out to doctors or a store, where I have to go. Of course, now it don't make a whole lot of difference, because I'm dying, so I won't have to worry about that anymore. That's the first thing I thought—"Gee, what a relief. I won't have to worry about going away anymore."

. . .

It wasn't too hard for me to leave my first husband. Like I said, there were times when I would get a little better, and since I was having so much trouble, it was easier to leave than to stay there with him. And then I met my second husband right away, so it wasn't too hard.

My second husband used to be a friend of my first husband. We got married, and then he got sick and got disabled, so he was home all the time. So I didn't have no trouble staying alone then, but I still had trouble going away. But he wasn't one that cared too much about going away anyway, so our marriage worked out fine.

My second husband died twelve years ago. I was scared when he died, because I thought I wouldn't be able to stay alone. But it hasn't been that bad. In fact, I don't think I could live with anybody. . . .

I don't get out much now. Mostly just to the doctors and to the store, and usually my son takes me. And I get out around the house here and visit with a couple of the neighbors now. It's not as bad as it used to be. But if I have to go anywhere strange . . . . Of course, I haven't been out of the house too much since I got this. It's just been a couple weeks since I've been home from the hospital.

When you left your first husband, did you just kind of sneak out?

How'd I do that? It was so long ago. Yeah, I think I had the neighbor girl come over and babysit, and I left while he wasn't home. I didn't have nowhere to take the kids. My mother was already dead. My dad, like I said, was remarried, and we didn't get along too good. But that probably was my fault—well, not exactly, but he was an alcoholic. And then, when I was molested by my grandfather, he didn't protect me when I told him about it. He just told me to keep quiet. So I kind of was resentful. . . .

I tried to protect myself all the time, by not being with [my grandfather] in the room alone or anything. And they said that's what caused me not to trust people.

When I left my first husband—it sounds terrible, but it wasn't as bad as it sounds—I went with my second husband. We stayed in a motel for a few days, and then after he got a job, we got married.

. . .

I have just one child that's still alive from my second marriage. He comes every day, he calls every day—he's just a couple miles away. His wife and he have a baby.

I had a couple others—one died when he was six weeks and the other was born in seven months, and he died. That's why I said it hasn't been a real good life here.

. . .

Now that I'm sick, everybody's treating me so good. It's really strange. Now I feel like somebody cares—like I'm special. But I don't know why they gotta wait until you're dying.

Is there anything in particular that's made you the happiest in your life?

The thing I think has made me the happiest is my little grandson. He'll be three in August. He really gives me a lot of pleasure, because they bring him over at least once a week for me to see, ever since he was born. And I babysit for him sometimes, when they want to go out. . . .

I don't know if there's any meaning or purpose to life. I have a feeling we're put here, and they already know when we're going to die. No matter what you do or don't do, you're going to die at a certain given time. . . . I just live from day to day, and take what comes. I don't really know.

When you were growing up, was there anything in particular you wanted to do or accomplish?

When I was young—before I started having all that trouble—I always wanted to be in politics, or work at a newspaper. But of course back then, it was harder for women to do. You was brought up to get married and have children, especially as a Catholic.

. . .

I was real, real religious—I used to pray so much for my mother and dad's alcoholism, and me getting molested, for all that to stop. And nothing ever happened—nothing ever got better. And slowly, I started pulling away. I figured, what's the use of praying? Nothing ever gets done anyway. You never get no help. But yet, I always believed in God. But I didn't go back to church for years. But now, I've gotten back into the Catholic church. And I do feel better being back in. But I still can't believe in prayer too much. I figure what's going to happen will happen whether you pray or not. . . .

I don't have any explanation for why the things that happened to me happened. I felt I was just born in the wrong family. When I was little, I always used to wish I belonged somewhere else. In fact, I remember when I was little, I thought they adopted me, because everything was so bad, I must have been adopted. But I never found no adoption papers, so I guess I wasn't.

Is there anything in your life that you wish you'd done differently?

Yes, I wish I'd found some way to take my first two kids with me when I left. I always felt guilty about that. Although after I explained everything to the therapist, and even a couple of my aunts, they said it wasn't my fault, the way things were. . . .

My therapist tells me I'm strong, or I couldn't have put up with all that. But to me, I always thought I was weak.

. . .

I have cancer of the colon. They operated, but they couldn't get it all. And then I got tumors on my liver.

. . .

One thing I have trouble with is, when anybody calls or comes over or anything, I come right out and say I'm dying. And boy, everybody shuts up or leaves. I can't see where that's wrong, but it seems like everybody gets scared when you say that. . . .

The first time they told me I might be dying, one doctor said I had four months to two years, and the other doctor said a year. At first, I didn't want to die, because I wanted to see my grandson grow up. And then there's things I wanted to do. I know they don't seem important, but I've got a lot of books here I wanted to read, and I make afghans, and I've got ten or twenty here that I wanted to make. And I know I won't get that done now. But now, I don't mind so much. I think, if I die now, at least I won't have to worry about nothing no more. All my pain will be gone.

The only thing that scares me is the end. I worry about the pain, when it gets close to the end. . . . But the hospice has told me they'd make sure I wasn't in pain. They've been real good, just like angels.

And even my church now, as long as I've been away from it, they cook all my meals, and bring me more food than I can eat. In fact, I've had to call and tell them not to bring so much, I've got too much here.

· · ·

Do you think there's a life after death?

Now there's another thing that bothers me. That's the other thing I'm scared of—not knowing what happens to you after you die. Is there a heaven, or do you just die and know nothing? Because nobody knows for sure. And that part scares me a little bit.

The religion hasn't really been helpful. Like I said, I believe in God, but yet I'm not sure about this after-death stuff. . . .

My attitude towards life hasn't really changed since I found out I had cancer. The only thing is, like I said, you wonder why everybody gets nice to you when you're dying. I guess it's just time for me to go.

Do you have any advice for other people about how they should live their lives?

Well, all I can say is, try to live the best that you can. I feel that, after a few mistakes I made when I was younger, I did okay. I didn't do nothing that shouldn't have been done. I think everybody makes mistakes when they're young. And when you get older, you think, "If I could live it over again, I'd do it different." But when you're young, you think you know everything.

· · ·

I think you should just accept death when they tell you. Don't be afraid. I was afraid for a few days, but my son is worse off than I am. He's having a hard time. But I'm kind of getting used to it now. A little scared at times. But I've accepted it, I think.

3

Support Systems:
Having a Place in the World

Support systems were one of the primary sources of happiness and contentment for many of the interviewees. Although family was often the most important component of such systems, others—such as friends, members of the community, and even nonhuman elements (such as pets or a home)—also played significant roles. A number of people said that support from family, friends, and others was essential in helping them cope with their illnesses, for it gave them the strength, as well as the desire, to continue on. Support systems also provided people with the comfort and security of knowing there was a place in the world where they were loved and accepted for who they were—a place where they belonged.

ELAINE SKIFFINGTON-BARNES
MOUNTAIN AREA HOSPICE

I live in Asheville, North Carolina. I come from a big Irish-Catholic family. I had seven brothers and sisters. We were raised in East Lansing, Michigan. We moved to a suburb of Chicago when I was in the fourth grade. I grew up there. I went to Southern Illinois University College. That's where I met my [first] husband. We got married in 1976. It was the year of the tall ships—I remember that. It was the bicentennial year. And then we moved to Florida. I had my first and only daughter in Florida. We lived in Ft. Myers, and we managed a hydroponic tomato farm. . . .

I didn't like being in southern Florida, away from my family and friends. A friend of ours suggested we try the mountains of western North Carolina, and that's where we ended up.

We came here when my baby was just a few months old, so it's been about fifteen years now.

. . .

I have four brothers and three sisters. I'm the fifth oldest of the children. I'm the youngest daughter. I liked having a big family. We always had a clan—always had a party or always had enough to play ball.

. . .

My brothers and sisters are spread out all around the world now. I have one in Europe, Costa Rica, Chicago and Florida. . . . We're all real close. . . . My dad passed away before my baby was born. I was pregnant, and I didn't know it.

My mom sold the house in Chicago and moved to Florida. And she's still there. . . .

I liked growing up in Chicago and Michigan—I'm a northern girl. I miss it. I miss the Great Lakes, and the north. I don't like the slow, take-it-easy lifestyle down here too much. It seems so passive. I'm used to more aggressive, assertive people. Everybody here's, "Yeah, I'll think about it for a few months, a few years." So time is just kind of endless down here. It's hard for me, being a Yankee. And everybody knows I'm a Yankee, even after fifteen years. They say, "You're not from around here, are you?"

But my daughter loves it down here. It's beautiful up in the mountains.

My second husband is from Charlotte, North Carolina, and he's lived there all his life. So there's no way we would move. He always wanted to live in the mountains, so he moved here.

I remarried six years ago. And dag, two months later, I was in the hospital for a radical hysterectomy for cervical cancer. . . . Then I had surgery again about a year and a half later. That helped me about a year, and then it was apparent that it was coming back again. I tried two different series of chemo, but it didn't work either. And then, buyin' time, buyin' time. By then I'd quit my job—retired is what I say. . . . Retired at thirty-seven.

I ended up in the hospital because the tumor blocked my bowels, and I had a colostomy put in. I recovered from that. I went downhill. I had chemo last August. After that, I didn't get much stronger—I got worse. By Christmastime, my doctor had mentioned having a pelvic exoneration [a type of operation]. I wasn't even a good candidate for it. There's a twenty to twenty-five percent chance of non-survival. By January, I went in his office and said, "Do something." Because the tumor was pressing on my leg and my spine, and I couldn't walk or anything like that. At the end of January of this year, I went in and had it done, and I'll be danged if I didn't make it through all right. I would have taken either route. So I've been recuperating from that surgery. But in the meantime, I just had another little surgery last week, because the darn tumor keeps showing up. . . . Oh, and when I had the pelvic exoneration, they took away my bladder, and so now I have a urostomy tube—there's another name for it, but that's what I call it. And today, I'm going in for a CAT scan, because it looks like they're going to have to go back.

. . .

It was hard having to go through all those treatments. Most of the time, I'm up, but right now, I'm down. It's hard to be in the hospital all the time. But I have a great support system in town. It's my network support system and my big family that turn me on—help is just a phone call away.

Developing my spirituality has been the biggest help to me. I didn't even start seeing that side—that void in my life—until a year and a half ago. I got involved in a real upbeat church. Then I went back to a real traditional church, but a very open traditional church. I met this wonderful lady who's a graduate of Duke Divinity School. We have a women's group that meets every other week. We meet by candlelight and hang around, and pray, and do all sorts of fun stuff. And developing that side of me has really been the key for me. Because before that, I was angry, and frustrated and fighting. Now, I'm probably still angry, and I'm probably still frustrated, but if I can go within myself and pray or meditate, it's a lot easier. . . .

After all the surgeries, radiation, and all this crap, I guess I'm here . . . I'm not sure why I'm here, to tell you the truth. I fought the odds, and I'm here, but I always say I don't even know . . . well, nobody knows how much longer, or why I'm one of these ones that . . . I think it's because I'm young—or I was young. I'm going to be forty this year. You bounce back pretty quickly when you're young.

. . .

After they did the procedure in January, they said, "Oh, we're sure we bought you at least one or two years." So I got all optimistic, and my family got all optimistic.

45

But one or two years of what? I forgot to ask that part.

*How do you deal with it when the doctors say you
only have a certain amount of time left?*

I'm not sure. I'm real stubborn—the French/Irish background. First, I get depressed. And then, all I have to do is look
at my daughter, and I want to keep going. I think having her
has been . . . I've been really grateful. . . . I guess just looking
at my family, or coming home and being around my house,
and my dog—I just forget about death sentences, and nest with
what I've got. Then it doesn't matter. The one day at a time
thing is so overused and trite, but it really works. It's real hard
to do that, though. You have to practice that.

Our society doesn't really honor that. We honor yesterday
and the future, but it seems to me that we don't really go with
the present. . . . Our culture is, "Hurry up, hurry up. Give it to
me now." Instant gratification. It's been hard, because you
don't get that in my situation.

. . .

You keep trying to find someplace where you feel safe,
and feel that your prayers will be heard, if not answered. Because, sitting at home, with no community outreach, and no
contact, and no network, I definitely wouldn't be here. If you
take away my family, and my community, and hospice, and
doctors who'll let you cry in their office—no way. I guess that's
all the positive stuff in my life.

*What are the things that have made you the happiest
in your life?*

Oh boy. . . . I guess the typical answer for a mother—my
daughter. The outdoors—I love Mother Nature. I'm a gardener.
Fooling around with plants and flowers, and landscaping. I
love landscaping. Working with my hands makes me happy. I

46

like to do just about anything with my hands—I like to sew. I cook a little bit. In my better days, I liked to cook. I like to travel. I like to visit my family all around the world.

I don't know . . . I don't know how to say it. I wish I could say my marriages, but I don't want to be negative about it. I'm not an easy person to be married to, I think. Plus, I'm putting my second husband through hell, with being ill from the start. We were happy together when we could go hiking in the Blue Ridge Mountains every weekend. We were real happy with that. We did that, probably the first four years of our marriage. Now, we just kind of daydream about it a lot, and remember. That's what we like to do together. . . .

I didn't have any idea when I was a kid what I wanted to do when I grew up. I grew up in the wild '70s, late '60s. I was a rebel without a cause—one of those kids. I wanted to buck the establishment, buck society, buck anything organized. I left home quite early—straight out of high school—and took off, and lived with a rock 'n roll band. I drove my poor parents crazy.

I never really was career-oriented. Actually, I always got the impression that the women were raised to be good Catholic wives, and have children, and some guy is going to take care of you. That's why I'm so grateful to have a daughter, to tell her, "Hey, there isn't some prince out there that's going to rescue you and take care of you for the rest of your life, and you're going to be a lady of leisure."

I kind of missed that whole career thing. I've been to three or four colleges, and tried different things, but I really think I'm more of an artist/naturalist-type. I tried legal school, I tried nursing school, I tried state university, but none of them were me. . . . But I kind of regret bucking society and all, because it's a lot easier when you go along with it, follow the program. We don't have any money, we don't have any stocks or bonds or savings. We're just making it, day by day.

But I've got a dog, and I've got a house, and a husband that sticks with me, though I don't know why.

. . .

*Do you think there's any particular meaning or pur-
pose to life?*

Yeah, I'm sure there is. Yes. You have to be true to yourself, and be the best with what you are given. I really believe
that you should use your gifts and your talents wisely. Everyone's unique, everyone's different, and we've been given different skills. I feel if you take care of yourself, and be the best
you can be . . . .

We can't solve world hunger by ourselves, or world peace,
but I really believe it begins in your heart, with one individual.
And that if you're true to yourself, and love yourself, you can
accomplish great things.

❧

PETER ALLEGRI
HOSPICE CARE OF THE VISITING NURSE ASSOCIATION

I'm forty-two years old. I grew up here in Kansas City, Missouri. I had four brothers. I lost two of them a couple years
ago—one got killed and the other died of cancer. My mom
died July 4 [1993]. I have a sister. I was in the middle—I had
two older and three younger.

. . .

I worked in restaurants and bars all my life. I managed
restaurants and bars. I liked dealing with people. My brother
owns a bar and restaurants, and that's how I got into it.

. . .

I'm not married—I'm living with a guy. . . . I first realized I was gay when I was twenty-six. It wasn't a surprise when I realized it. I knew it mostly all my life. I had a feeling I was. But raising up in an Italian family, you had to be a little careful. And I decided to come out, so I did.

Coming out was difficult, but it wasn't. I have a good family, and they support me real good. . . . They always were there for me, so it was a lot easier to come out than I thought it would be. My friends accepted it; my brothers' friends too. They all know, and they're all Italians—big Italians. They accepted it too. So it was a lot easier.

I had a lot of girlfriends when I was a kid. I even was married once. It was when I was twenty-two, I think. I lived with her for four years.

. . .

I went to Chicago and I met a friend, and he helped me come out. He made me feel comfortable—he made me feel I was as good as anyone else. I felt that my family would either love me the way I was or they don't love me at all. But they loved me. . . .

They weren't really surprised when they found out. They knew it. They kind of were waiting for me to come out and tell it. They had ideas when I was growing up.

. . .

I found out I had HIV about seven, eight years ago. I felt real bad. I felt real funny when I was at work—weak. So I went to a doctor, and she told me.

I took it real well, because I knew I had it. So it was easier when she told me—it didn't bother me as much. I lived life one day at a time anyway.

Other people weren't too shocked when I told them I had it. They took it pretty easy. First, I told my little brother, and he didn't seem to be too shocked over it. Then he went ahead and told my older brother, and next, my whole family knew. But

49

they were always real supportive for me. They always were standing by me.

But I wasn't expecting to lose my mom and my two brothers. I thought I was going to die before them. It seems like everybody around me is dying before I am.

. . .

I've been with hospice for six months. And they didn't think I would make it this long. I shocked the hell out of all of them.

I feel pretty good right now. The last couple days I've been feeling pretty good. It comes and goes. Every other day I get sick for a couple days, and then I feel real good, and then I'm sick. It all depends on what day it is.

. . .

I'm not very active at all now. I wear out real easy. If I go out and do something one day, it takes me a week to recover. So I stay home and watch tv a lot, and keep home and relax.

My nurse comes by three times a week. She's a real good nurse—she's a doll.

I got a lot of friends living in the apartment building, so we go back and forth to their apartments. And they're all sick too, so it's easy to be around them. But you have to be careful— we have more chance of catching something from somebody else than they do from us. So usually I try to keep away from people who have colds or whatever, because if not, I could get sick as hell. I've been in the hospital about twenty times now, with pneumonia. I should have been dead a long time ago. But I've been lucky. . . .

Mentally, I've been dealing with it pretty good. My family's all up there waiting for me, so I'm not afraid of dying. Sometimes I wonder why it's taking so long. Because I've been at death's door a couple times, where I couldn't even get out of bed or walk.

During those times, I'd wonder if I was going to make it,

or die. Don't know if I am or not. But they put me on medication and I pop right back up.

I don't know why I've been able to stay healthy. Because I've been real sick, and then I'm real healthy again. And my friends would say, "God, last time I saw you, you looked like you was dead. And now you look real good." I've outlived a lot of people—I've lost about twenty friends in maybe a year, with the virus. . . .

I don't plan anything, because you never know what's going to happen. A lot of my friends who were looking good, and I didn't think were sick, I'd turn around and next week they're dead. You never know—I could be dead next week, if it hits me that fast. I don't plan anything, because every time I plan something, I end up in the hospital. . . .

Me and my roommate would like to go to the ocean—he never saw the ocean, and he wants to see that before he dies. We're going to try to go in a couple months. . . . He's into whales. We want to go somewhere where we can see the whales. Then he would be happy, and I would be happy.

Do you believe there's a heaven or a hell?

I believe in heaven, yes. I definitely believe in a heaven. I don't know about the hell yet. But living is hell. I believe there's another country up above. That's why I never really moaned too much about my family dying, because to me, they ain't dead—they're on vacation, and I'm going to join them later. . . . And I lost a lover four year ago, too. He's been dead four years now. I'm buried next to him. I got my funeral lot, with my name on my grave. So I'm pretty set. I'm very easy about death, because I never worried about it—if I die, I die. But I do keep the faith—I do believe in God.

I was raised pretty religious. My mom's very Catholic, and she brought us up in a Catholic family.

What are the things that have made you the happiest?

51

Living, I guess, and having fun. I had a lot of happiness being around my family. I loved going over there on holidays. I love going out and talking to people, and seeing people. That makes me happy. . . .

I don't think there's any particular meaning or purpose to life. To me, I don't have no purpose in life. I don't want to plan everything—I live from one day to another. I take life as it comes. When it's time to go, I'm going to be ready. . . .

There's nothing in my life I wish I'd done differently. Nothing I wouldn't do over again. I'm happy for what I am. I'm happy being gay, because I met a lot of different people, and a lot of wonderful people. . . . I've been lucky with friends. All my friends who know I'm gay accept me as I am. So that's pretty good.

. . .

I don't think about death. I enjoy my life while I got it now, and do the best that I can.

❧

GENE RELFORD
ST. VINCENT HOSPICE

I grew up in Indianapolis. I was born here. I'm sixty-two years old. I had polio when I was ten years old. From there, it went into rheumatoid arthritis. I've sort of been handicapped, but I've tried to overcome it, and I've been able to get the job done most of my life. I founded a company, and I've been pretty self-sufficient.

My health started failing as I got older. I sold my company to a company that had the same customer base—they were in the fuel-related business, and I was in electrical. They agreed to keep me on as a consultant, and I said I'd continue working until I couldn't work anymore. We don't have control over those things, unfortunately.

The way I started my own business was, nobody emphasized the need for education—in my part of the world anyhow—for handicapped people in those days. I just kind of got in on a service station job. Then I knew I had to specialize in something, so I started specializing in carburetors in automobiles. I got pretty good at that, but I could see that carburetion was coming to—that there was something better out there than that. So I got into electrical, and I really liked that. I started working on putting my business together, and it took me about five years. I got it together in 1969. It involved starters and alternators for heavy-duty construction and agricultural equipment. . . .

We built a lot of race car starters for the Indy 500. We helped develop some of that for some of the bigger names in racing.

. . .

I contracted polio because it's a virus, and they didn't have the vaccine then. It usually got you on one side or the other. It affected me on the right side—my right arm and right leg. It was kind of a bad time, because it was right at the start of World War II, and all the doctors had been drafted into the Army, so nobody really knew what to do. My mom did the best she could. They put you up on pillows, and didn't try to exercise you or keep your joints limber. As a result, I had a lot of joints that froze up. That kind of plagued me over the years. But I worked around it pretty good.

I've led a pretty good life. I worked every day, and I did normal . . . well, normal for me—I couldn't play sports or anything. I was married for a number of years. I worked, and did a lot of things that a lot of people do. All in all, I had a real good life.

Did people treat you differently because of the polio?

Well, I'm short—I'm only five feet tall. The polio stopped the growth of my long bones—my thigh bones and arm bones. There's a few people in my business who look at the world through the paper towel roll or whatever, and don't recognize that this is what a man looks like or this is what a woman looks like. So there was a little bit of that in my life. But there was a lot more of the other—a lot more people who remembered me and were kind to me because of it.

When I was a kid, I really didn't know what I would do when I grew up. My mom was a real good person, and encouraged me to do anything I wanted to do. Unfortunately, she didn't have any education, and it wasn't a big important thing to her. I just sort of rambled along.

I went to the ninth grade. Then I started working in a little print shop. I didn't really like that. I was always interested in cars, so I got involved in that.

. . .

I had five brothers and four sisters. . . . I had three brothers and two sisters older than me, and two brothers and two sisters younger than me. It was kind of nice having a big family. We were sort of poor, but we had enough. My dad was a glazier, a contractor. During World War II he started making a decent salary. We had a good amount to eat. Nothing fancy, but we had enough.

. . .

I was married for about twenty-five years. It didn't work out real well. I was about twenty-three or twenty-four when I got married. I think when I got married, a lot of my friends had started getting married, and I thought that was what I wanted to do too. And I think she did too. But it really wasn't. . . .

We didn't have any children.

. . .

*What are the things that have made you the happiest
in your life?*

Well, I think my friends. I tried to be a good friend all the
time. I just went all out to be a friend, without asking for anything in return. And I've loved a lot of people that are maybe
off-color to somebody else—that have shady sides to them. But
I think they've got a lot of solid gold in them. I've been absolutely open about that, and I've never been afraid to express
it. And that has come back just a thousand times. I have some
of the neatest friendships and support group. A lot of them are
young people, and a lot are older people. And a lot of young
kids. And a lot of young people bring their kids. I have a lot
of kids' pictures here. . . .

I met a lot of these people through a place called the White
River Yacht Club. I started out with some conservation pro-
grams, teaching kids how to fish, and teaching them environmental things. The Yacht Club provided facilities and economic
assistance and boats for us. They were so nice, and they said,
"Well, how about helping us in our club here?" I did, and I became involved with them, and it's like a great big extended
family. There's about three or four hundred people that really
support me—young and old.

On August 13, we're having a kids' fishing tournament. I
have kind of mixed emotions this year. I brought some people
in to keep it going, and they're re-naming it in my honor. I feel
kind of guilty about it, and I feel kind of honored too. If they
keep that going, I'll still be part of the Yacht Club, and it'll still
be part of me. . . .

I've been involved with the Yacht Club for about fifteen
years. We do three of those kids' fishing things. We have one
strictly for inner-city kids, and it's called Friends of White River.
We have one called the Family Fishing Association. It's a very

positive program—every kid who competes gets a trophy. We say we don't have any losers. So everyone can walk away feeling good. . . .

I got involved in conservation initially because my dad always took me fishing as a kid. That was one thing he could do—he could take me fishing. We'd sit on the bank there. He liked to fish. . . . It became very important to me.

I like kids. I think, probably because I'm little, they kind of relate to me too. I try to treat them like people. That's what they tell me: "You always treated me like a person, instead of a kid."

Do you keep up with people you dealt with when they were kids?

Yeah. When I go to a shopping center I'll see a kid. Of course, they're grown now—I'd never have recognized them. And they expect me to remember the fish they caught. Like I said, I'm kind of memorable looking—like a Looney Tunes cartoon character. They don't realize they've all changed—they're heads taller.

But it's fun. I have real good memories of it.

Do you think there's any particular meaning or purpose to life?

Yeah. When you're sitting here, it's just your love, your family and your friends. That's what it is. It doesn't make any difference how much money I made, or what my title was. It doesn't make any difference. I can sit here and feel peace and security. I feel like, the love I get back, I get from different places. I could have fallen in love with my second grade teacher, and she could have never known it, but I can get love back now, today, and it feels just as good. You don't have to get it back from the same person. I think that's a big plus for me. I feel a lot of love from people. And I think part of that's because I've been willing to share it. It is kind of a hard thing to do, because you take a risk of exposing yourself to ridicule or rejection. I've tried to overcome that. And it's hurt. Probably if I had one misgiving in my life, I'd probably felt that I'd loved a lot more than I'd gotten. But since I've been [in the hospice], I've changed that, because I know that I've gotten back a hundred times more than I've given.

These people [in the hospice] are just like a family to me. They just can't do enough for you. They do everything they can to help you. They just do it absolutely, and they're just pleased to do it. . . . They just accept you unconditionally.

. . .

[Mr. Relford had just completed radiation treatments for a brain tumor and a lung tumor. He first found out about the lung tumor in March of 1992, and learned about the brain tumor more recently.]

I fell in my apartment, and laid there for three days, so they brought me here. They thought I'd had a stroke or something. They looked to see what happened, and found the brain tumor.

I guess I was surprised when I found out about the brain tumor. I knew my health was failing. . . . But it's not scary— it's sort of peaceful, knowing that I'm doing everything I can do, and they're doing everything they can do. I thank God I didn't lie on the floor and die, because I've gotten to see all the friendship and love. I'm grateful for that.

Do you have any advice for other people about how they should live their lives?

Well, I think you just have to go balls-out for love. That's all that makes any difference. Anything else doesn't make any difference. It's a powerful emotion, because it feels so good, and yet can hurt so bad at the same time. But certainly for me, it's been well worth it—the good part overshadows the bad. . . . It really doesn't make any difference if you had a million bucks. You couldn't shovel any of that in your casket. But you sure can take that love with you.

4

Religion

Religion was an integral part of many of the interviewees' lives, providing a sense of order and meaning. Their belief that there is a purpose behind everything that occurs, or even simply that there is a benevolent God, was a source of great comfort and helped them cope with the hardships they faced. In addition, those who believed in a life after death seemed to face the prospect of their own deaths with greater equanimity than those who did not. Although different people had different conceptions of what the afterlife would be like, many believed (or at least hoped) they would be reunited with those they had loved and lost here on earth. Moreover, even those who were uncertain as to what heaven was like firmly believed it would be a better place than that in which we currently live.

GEORGETTE

CABRINI HOSPICE

[Georgette is in her fifties.]

I was born and raised right here in Brooklyn. . . . I was raised in the tougher part of Brooklyn. . . . I went to Pennsylvania for three years in between. I lived there for three years, from when I was eleven until I was fourteen. I came back because I missed my brothers and my sister. I didn't like having a better life with my aunt and uncle, and they were stuck here with my grandmother. I felt that they were having problems, the way I always had problems with her. You know, my parents didn't raise us, my grandmother raised us.

When I had left to go visit my aunt and uncle, I asked them if I could stay, because I didn't like the life here very well. I had it nice [in Pennsylvania]; I had a home, a private house, with a typical tree in the yard, and a porch to sit on. And I felt guilty that my sister and my brothers had nothing here. My aunt and uncle wanted to adopt me, but I didn't feel right—that I should have a better life, and they have nothing.

. . .

I don't remember too much [about Pennsylvania], except that it was nice. I went to a nice school, with nice kids for a change. I had a nice life there—you know, your typical country girl's story. It would have been for me had I been an only child. But being one of four, being plucked off the streets of Brooklyn, and leaving the others behind, I just . . . I just couldn't live with it. When it came down to the nitty gritty, my guilty feelings kept me from saying, "Yes," and signing the [adoption] papers. And I said I wanted to come home.

. . .

Childhood was kind of rough. It was a little on the rough side. And that's about it. I got married. I basically married a man who was a friend of mine. And my main reason was to get out of the house. Because once I came home from Pennsylvania, I realized it was the wrong thing to do. . . . My grandmother was rough. Very rough. She was a very prejudiced lady. I had cared for a young fella who was Cuban, and she destroyed that for me. So in essence, when I married, I had no room for loving somebody. But my husband at the time wanted to marry and take chances, and I figured, "Okay, fine." I was eighteen when I got married. But it didn't last, because you don't marry without caring. It never works.

But I got something wonderful out of it—I had my son. So some good comes out of things. So it was meant to be.

. . .

So that was my earlier part of my life. And after that, it was just work, and trying to make my life better from that point on. Which I did. It worked out nice. I had a nice life.

When I met my honey [her second husband], my life began. At that time, I was twenty-four. That's when I was born. . . . And that was it. That was my whole life. Him, my son—that was about it. They were everything. They kept me happy.

. . .

God has given me a good twenty-seven, twenty-eight years with this man. And it's helped me to grow. I've grown into a person. He was not only my husband at home, he was my best friend, my father I never had, my mother I never had. He was everything as far as that goes. . . . We never became abundantly wealthy, and things like that, because it's a tough life, and he never was that healthy. He never had that stamina to do what he might have wanted to do.

. . .

If you want to know, as far as, say people have reasons for living; when they say their reason for living has been their family, their kids . . . that's only part of being happy. What really makes you happy is your great belief in God Himself. That's really what has been my staff and my strength. . . . I always spoke to Him. Ever since I was a little girl, when I was unhappy, I used to go up on the roof of the big apartment building we lived in, and I used to go up and speak to Him. . . . And I always got feedback. It's not that you hear a voice coming at you, but you know someone is directing you. And I always felt it was Him. And that's been my utmost guidance. It's different—you have an earth love, and if we all listen to our guardian angel, that's the true feelings, the true reason to live. Because we're here for a reason. We're all here for a purpose. And when it's done, then God takes us to Him, to where we belong. I call it going home. He takes us home.

. . .

[Georgette described a near-death experience she had during a water skiing accident when she was in her early twenties.]

That's when I realized that we're here on earth to do certain things, but we live elsewhere. My soul was in another spot. Like an out-of-body experience. The only thing is, I didn't go through a tunnel and see light—I just was in a garden. I was just there, like I belonged. . . . Then everything made sense to me. It all made sense. Whatever happened to me— my grandmother, the years with her, the years with my sister and brothers—it's all meant to be. It's written. Somewhere, it's in your slate. And no matter what we do, it's going to happen. It's not our life. Our life is elsewhere. Here, we're just doing a job, the way you go to work, and punch your time card. Every day we wake up, we're punching a time card on the job we have to do here on earth. And we have to learn certain things in order to go on, to maybe another dimension, or plateau, or whatever. The way you study to go on in college. . . . When our jobs are done, then God takes us, no matter how old we are. We could be here a year, and our job has been done. And He takes us, and we go home.

I think that we're here because we want to be here. . . . We choose to come back and make up, because no one's perfect. So we have to clean that slate. We have to make good, and we want to make good, because you can't go on to the next plateau unless you clean your slate for something wrong that you've done.

. . .

That's when I started to think that everything made sense to me. Ever since that one day. . . . Like when I met my [second] husband, I just knew. I didn't want to meet him. I wasn't interested, I couldn't be bothered, had my own problems. I didn't even see the man. I just saw the back of him. And I just knew this was my Waterloo. And as fast as I thought, "Get out of there, go back, go outside," that's how fast he turned around. And I felt bad to say, "Hello, goodbye." . . . And my girlfriends had set it up—that I would be home that weekend, that I'm dying to meet him. That's all the lies they told him. They didn't say a word to me, because they knew I would never show. But I knew in my heart and soul that God directed him to me, no matter how he looked. He was heavyish—I didn't want somebody heavy. He was hairy—I didn't want somebody hairy. . . . And at that time, I was twenty-four years old—I was in pretty good shape. [Laughs.] He was older than me. And I didn't want any part of this. And I'm thinking, "This is not for me." But yet I knew in my heart and soul, that that's my life, no matter how I run from it. I've met it. So that's the way I say God directs us. Somehow, you just know.

. . .

I don't mean to get religious. I'm not a religious person, in a formal sense. I don't go to church on Sundays. . . . I don't even know a prayer right through. . . . But I don't run away, and I don't do things to offend. Like the way you don't disrespect your father. I don't disrespect. The way you would love your family—your mother and father come first—that's the way I love our Lord.

· · ·

[Georgette's second husband had died about a year earlier. Georgette found out she had cancer about the same time her husband became ill.]

That's why I'm thinking that my job is done, that maybe my honey was the reason . . . my reason was to have helped him in his life. To understand life, to understand different people. To help bring love in his heart. Because he was misunderstood, always, as a tough man. He wasn't. And I gave him unconditional love. He didn't have to be rich, he didn't have to be earning a good salary. If he had a dollar, we managed on a dollar. If he had a hundred dollars, we managed on a hundred. I didn't push him into anything that he couldn't handle. So I gave him unconditional love. And since God has taken him, his job is done. He did a wonderful job raising my son. And loving me. I used to pray to God only that He send me somebody to truly love me. Not to give me. Just to truly love me, for me, like a parent would. And He's given me that. So my honey did his part. And in turn, through the years, now my part is done. So that might have been my reason.

I'm trying to piece it together. I don't want to ask God, "Why me, Lord?" I never asked, "Why me?" I just asked my Lord to give me strength for whatever He is giving me. Just to give me strength to bear whatever He does put on me, to help me through it.

· · ·

My daughter-in-law is a wonderful girl. And that's another thing God directed. And I know it's God directing, because He knows He's taking me. He sends my son a wife who is so much like me, it's as if I'll never be dead as long as she's alive. And now my little granddaughter, I see so much of myself in her. So it's never that I'm going to be gone from them. So they don't need me. All they have to do is just look at each other. All my son has to do is keep loving his wife, and he sees his mom in her, and his little one, and he's never alone.

Whereas with me now, even though they are my living reason to live . . . . Say God all of the sudden decides, "I'm going to take this horrible tumor and throw it away like a basketball, and give her another chance." Then they become my reason to get up in the morning, to go to work—to do. Because you need somebody on earth to make you smile, and to fulfill. . . . You still need it to put that smile on your face, that contentment in the earth-body. Because we live a tough life here. And we need something to give us pleasure.

. . .

It hasn't been easy, but it's been a nice life.

. . .

I'm looking forward to this death that I'm facing, because I'm really looking forward to going home. I'm looking forward to when God will take me, because I want to go home. I want to rest. I want that happiness again. And I'm not afraid.

❧

CLAUDE MICHAEL MURPHY
HOSPICE OF OKLAHOMA COUNTY

I'm forty-six years old. I live in Oklahoma City. I was born in Kansas City, Missouri, but I was raised in Oklahoma. I grew up, the elementary years, in Bartlesville, Oklahoma. High school years were spent at Fairfax, Oklahoma. I went to bible college and got a degree. And then I went into maintenance work, because I did not feel called to the ministry. This was back during the Vietnam War. It made a big difference in things.

I went into maintenance work. I started out as a department maintenance man and I worked my way up to chief engineer of a ninety-three bed psychiatric hospital. And that was too much pressure—I started to feel like I was cracking up, so I went back down the ladder a few notches and stayed in the same field, but went to work for the state of Oklahoma.

. . .

I had gone to college with the plan of going into the ministry, but this was a very tight-knit denomination, and there were no openings. When I graduated, there was no possibility of becoming a minister in that denomination. And changing denominations at that time was unthinkable. Since then, I have pretty much changed my religious beliefs. I'm more of a mainstream Christian now. Back in those days, I was more of a very, very strict fundamentalist. . . . I had discovered that denomination through radio preaching when I was in high school.

. . .

I enjoyed parts of the college experience, but I did not enjoy other parts of it. Like I said, they were very, very strict, and it seems like I was always butting heads with the authorities.

My religious beliefs are different now. I threw away all the literature. There was voluminous literature, much like the Jehovah's Witnesses. And I started reading the New Testament, just by itself, and I discovered that they were way off the beam in their strictness and their minute control of individuals' lives.

. . .

I'm an only child, and I'm adopted.

My father's still alive. He'll be sixty-eight this year. My mother died in 1990. And an interesting story here is, I started looking for my birth parents, and I found my birth mother in 1991.

I had started looking for my birth parents in 1969, and all the doors were closed at that time. In 1991, I joined an adoption search group, and they gave me some leads. And then I found out my birth mother was from the state of Kansas, and Kansas is very liberal in giving out adoption information. So I wrote to the Department of Vital Statistics, and they sent me her birth certificate. And then I found out she was from the same town as my adoptive parents had relatives. They contacted the school, and through a reunion book, they found out her current address, and I called her up.

At first, she denied it, but yet she was interested. So I could tell that she was the one. We had a nice ten minute conversation, and I said, "Would you like to take down my name and address?" And she said, "Yes." And I said, "Now you don't think you're my birth mother?" And she said, "Oh, no." But the fact that she wanted my name and address gave it away. And about three days later, she sent me a long letter and said, "Yes, I am the one, and I've been wondering about you for years."

And then in 1992, we got together. She came to see me and we spent a week together. It was very nice.

We still keep in touch regularly, by mail.

Did she explain the circumstances of what happened?

Yes, it was very strange. She had been raped by a member of the armed forces, and she got pregnant. . . .

She has other children. She had three daughters, and two of them are dead.

. . .

It must have been frustrating to be searching for that long.

Well actually, in 1969, after I found the doors were closed, I gave up. From the time I started the second time, it only took me six weeks. That was because of the change in the legal climate, plus I had the help of the adoption search agency. . . .

During that time, it was always in the back of my mind. You really wonder who you are, and do you have any brothers or sisters. It's kind of a big chunk of your life.

Since I found her, I feel much more at peace. I've gotten lots of pictures. When she came here, we went back up to Kansas where she lived, and we went to the cemeteries where all her relatives are buried. We just had a really nice time. I feel like I've got roots now. . . .

My adoptive parents are very supportive. My mother's dead; she was dead when I did this search, but my father's been very supportive.

. . .

Is there anything in particular that's made you the happiest in your life?

Yes, I would say it's been my relationship with Christ. And I have a great love of the New Testament. . . . That gives me comfort. It makes me feel like I've got eternal roots, I guess you could say. And I believe that Christians have eternal life. I'm very, very thankful that I was grounded in this before I found out I had terminal cancer.

Are there any times in your life that stand out as being especially good or not so good?

Yes, up until I found out I had cancer, I would say the decade before that has been the best. I had a job that I really, really liked, and all that time I was studying the New Testament—studying the Greek language, which it was originally written in. I don't know, I just felt like those were the best. Because you know, a job is very important. If you have a job that you don't like, and you spend eight hours a day doing it and you hate it, it's just awful.

I liked my job because I was able to work by myself. I was the 4:00 to 12:00 plant operator at a state building. And it was just very nice. I'm kind of a loner, and I enjoyed being by myself, and I didn't have any hassle, because everybody else went home at 4:30, when I came to work. And I had some free time at work, and I could study the Greek language, and I just really enjoyed it.

. . .

Do you think there's any particular meaning or purpose to life?

Yes, I believe we're put here on earth to come to a relationship with Christ and to devote our lives to Him, in His service. And I believe that qualifies us for eternal life. I'm very much a believer in the New Testament, but I do not believe that it's meant to be used to beat other people over the head with.

Is there anything in your life that you wish you'd done differently?

Yes, I wish I hadn't gotten involved in the [fundamentalist religious group]. . . . It was a learning experience, but it was very hard, because after I graduated, I had a bible college degree, but

70

I couldn't find a job. So I had to go back and do something that a person who came right out of high school could do, without any education whatsoever. And I didn't make much money for about five years. My wife and I lived in poverty. . . .

I didn't think about going back to school because I didn't have the money. I had a son—a young child, and it was against church policy for women to work outside the home. So I really had no opportunity to go back to school.

Do you have any advice for other people about how they should live their lives?

Well, I think everybody should be a Christian.

What do you think the consequences are of not being a Christian?

Well, the Bible says that if you do not have a grip on God, the result is hell. I can't argue with it if the Bible says it.

. . .

I found out I had cancer on April 14, last year. . . . I was shocked, because I've always been in excellent health. . . .

Now I feel very weak. . . . I was told by my doctor that I would just get gradually weaker and weaker. I'm not in a lot of pain, and I'm thankful for that.

. . .

Knowing I have this illness has affected the way I view life. I would say it's made each day a lot more valuable. Before, the days would sort of all run together, and I'd kind of get in a rut, where I wouldn't really look forward to any particular day—it was just going to be like the rest of them. But now, each one of them that comes along, I just try to live it to the fullest.

71

Do you have any particular idea of what heaven is like?

I read something one time that made a great impression on me. It was a story of an early doctor who went to see a man who was dying. He brought his dog with him to make the house call. He left the dog outside and he went in, and the dog was scratching and whining at the door. And the guy inside was afraid to die. He said, "I'm afraid to die, because I don't know what it's going to be like." But he wasn't Christian. And the Christian doctor said, "You hear that dog out there, scratching and whining because he wants to get in here? That dog doesn't know what it's like in here at all. But he wants to be in here because I'm here. That's the same way it is with us Christians. We want to be wherever Christ is."

That story made a great, great impression on me. If Christ is there, it's good enough for me.

❧

THOMAS SZALKIEWICZ
CABRINI HOSPICE

[Mr. Szalkiewicz is in his mid-thirties.]

I was born in Boston, Massachusetts. Third son of Elizabeth and Joseph. My mother is ethnic Irish; my father is an ethnic Pole. I went to grade school. At the age of fourteen, I went to trade school to learn to be a baker. But I took an IQ test, and I scored almost two hundred on it. So my principal advised me to go on to college. So I went on to prep school first, and from there I got a full scholarship to NYU for four years for pre-med.

I ended up changing my major from pre-med to French literature. . . . I ended up getting my degree from City College in
dramatic arts.

Then somehow I got a job proofreading for a publisher,
and that got more importance. I started writing articles in science, and that got me more attention. My last year before I got
sick, I ran the show. I dealt with authors, editors and proof-
readers. That was a good job.

I chose that field because I had a high verbal quotient. I
mean, I could always write, and I was a good writer, so I figured I'd exploit my talents.

I liked my job a lot. It's a shame I got sick, because I would
have stayed with it.

. . .

I started taking communion again. I have a prayer to St.
Jude, the patron saint of the hopeless cases. So I'm back on the
track of religion. I just started getting back the past month. I finally recognized that I need help. You know, I'm scared. My
level of immune cells is very, very low . . . and I'm frightened.

I have a skin problem now, and they say it's chiggers, but
I don't know. . . . Usually with AIDS, one of the first symptoms
you have, which is probably true throughout, is you usually get
skin problems first. And they indicate that the immune system
is not fighting.

That's just starting for me now—the beginning of the end.

. . .

I had communion five times this week. I think that I should
shore myself up as much as possible. If I die, I want to die in
a state of grace.

I think the religion helps—it gives me more strength. One
of the things that a woman who was here this week told me,
she said, "Hand it over to God. You can't deal with this by yourself. Ask God for His help." And that's what I'm doing. . . . I'm

73

doing what that woman said. I'm putting it in Jesus' hands, and asking Him to do what He wants.

Maybe it doesn't really help, but I feel it does. It's changed my attitude about this disease. I hope, as I did before, that I'll overcome this.

. . .

What are the things in life that have meant the most to you?

Well, the writing has. It's taken almost all my energy. Last year, I spent the whole year on the writing. . . . The title is "Degrees of Love," and it recounts my experiences as a patient with AIDS, and how, through my spirituality, I was able to overcome this particular virus. And I thought, "You did it. Why don't you share this with other people who are sick?" So I set out to capture it, so that those who are sick like me have some hope. I hope it's not a Pyrrhic victory. Here I am telling people I'm cured, and then I get sick.

Is there anything else you can think of in your life that you . . . ?

No, that's been the most important thing. It's been my life. You'll find it's a whole different attitude that you develop when you get a fatal disease.

Are there any particular moments in your life that stand out?

No, not really. I don't have an exciting life. I wish I did.

. . .

I believe that God, when He closes a door, He opens a window somewhere. So although you can't get in the front door, you can find a window, and you can get in.

The most profound experience was when I discovered about my spiritual self, and I realized it's a power that can be exploited, or it can be ignored. So I thank the Lord that I have this power.

. . .

Is there anything in your life that you wish you'd done differently?

To quote Edith Piaf, "Non, je ne regrette rien." No, I don't regret a thing. I wish I had been more enterprising making money. But more important to me was the art. Art above all else. That's how I saw it.

. . .

Do you have any advice for other people?

Well, I say, "carpe diem," to use a good Latin phrase. Seize the day. My philosophy of life is that this is a gift, and you should not take it for granted. It's a sacred gift. Some people have scorn toward life. And although it's very difficult at times, I have to say that it has its just rewards. I believe you should conduct your life in such a way that you pay homage to what it is. . . .

My attitude towards life has changed a lot since I found out I had HIV. I tend not to cling to it as much. I've gotten to a point now where I'm more accepting of my demise. What else can I do? You know, outrageous fortune, like Hamlet talks about? Slings and arrows. I don't feel that way.

Do you think there's any particular meaning or purpose to life?

75

I think you find your own meaning, yourself. It's like the way things have happened in the past fifteen years, since I first had symptoms of the disease. It could have taken a very bad turn, but I mustered up all the spirituality that I could, and I kept myself from dying. . . . And I said, "Oh, you have a key." My philosophy is to try to prolong life. Because it is an adventure. I want to go through the whole adventure. . . .

I don't have any plans for the future. One step at a time; one day at a time. I don't make long term plans. Especially in my condition, I'd be foolish to start making long term plans, and then get sick. So it puts me in a unique position. . . .

I think there's a life after death. I don't have any particular cosmology. Nothing I imagine. I think that the most important thing that we find when we die is we find those people who left us—who died. That to me would be a wonderful experience, because I loved all those people who died from AIDS. . . . There were friends and lovers. Two lovers, and the rest, some very close friends. They all died.

※

SISTER MARGARET BETZ
ALLEGHENY HOSPICE

My family roots are Irish and German, and I think both of those had a profound impact on me. . . . I'm the second of five children. I'm fifty-eight years old. One sister, Bev, is just eleven months older than I. We were pretty inseparable growing up. Donalee is two and a half years younger, and my brothers, Bob and Richard, four and five years younger. So we were pretty close age-wise, and our family was close-knit. As I look at the struggles families have today, I realize that I come from a very wonderful family. We had our share of ups and downs, but none of the huge problems that afflict so many families today. I'm really grateful for that kind of beginning.

. . .

I was born in Akron, Ohio. When I was ten, my dad was transferred to Baltimore. . . . That was a very significant move for all of us. For me, it marked the beginning of what has become a lifelong passion for justice. It was in Baltimore that I was first introduced to the reality of poverty and injustice. . . .

It was before the civil rights movement, and everything was pretty much segregated. . . . I remember one time on a Sunday drive with my family, we came to a school which had a big link fence around it. The playground was pavement, but there were weeds growing up in between, and there were broken windows in the school. I was astonished. I asked my dad about it, and he told me that the black children went there. I said, "But why?" Remember, I was only ten. When dad tried to explain "separate but equal"—the law of the land at that time—I protested. "It might be separate, but it sure isn't equal." His response continues to challenge me to this day: "I know it isn't equal, Marg. We have to find ways to change that. Maybe when you grow up you can help to make things equal."

I give my dad a lot of credit. Conversations like that profoundly influenced the desires of my heart and the decisions that eventually followed.

. . .

From the time we moved to Baltimore, I knew that I wanted to work for the underdog. The best way that I saw to do that was through the church. . . . So I decided early on that I wanted to be a Sister. I knew I didn't want to teach in a school or nurse in a hospital. I wanted to find a way to help people who didn't have anybody else. I've been really fortunate, because in my years as a Sister I've been able to do a lot of different things. For five years, I worked with Hispanic youngsters in Southern California. Later, following the riots of 1968, I did community organizing with the Interfaith Centers for Racial Justice in Detroit. We worked to counter institutional racism in the media and in educational materials. When I lived in Denver, I visited prisoners in the county jail every week, and I became active in the Coalition Against the Death Penalty. I've also been active in Amnesty International for about twenty years. And for fifteen wonderful years I was campus minister to university students.

. . .

My parents were very supportive when I told them I wanted to be a Sister. Actually, they've been supportive to all five of us in whatever we've chosen to do. I think that's one of the things that made them really super parents. I chuckle as I remember—I must have been eleven or twelve—when my mom told me, "Now Margaret, you don't have to marry the first man who asks you. You do with your life what you want to do." And I remember thinking, "Oh! That's pretty nice!"

. . .

One of my sisters is a Sister. My older sister and two brothers married and have families. I love them and remain close to all of them. Now their children are growing up and some of them are marrying. It's kind of wonderful to see the life cycle continue that way.

. . .

I moved to Pittsburgh in 1989, and have been Pastoral Associate at St. Thomas More Parish here since July 1991. When I came to the parish, I was healthy. Less than a year later, though, I was diagnosed with ovarian cancer. Having been healthy all my life, learning that I had cancer came as a huge, devastating surprise. . . . It's been two years now. I've discovered that, along with all the grief, tears, anger and frustration, this cancer is really a gift to me and to the people of the parish.

It's part of our shared faith journey. Also, I'd never worked much with older people or sick people. I find that, being sick myself, I'm able to "be with" them in ways I might not have been able to before. So, strange as it may seem, cancer has become a very great blessing in my life.

Have you ever had second thoughts about whether you should be doing something else?

I suppose that if I had several lives to live, I might do something besides what I'm doing now. Like, I think it would be wonderful to be married and have a family. Although I've never had children of my own, I love children—all children. There are so many children around the world without the nurturing and love that they need and deserve. That saddens me deeply. And it angers me. I would like to give other children the kind of loving family life I had.

Sometimes I fantasize how wonderful it would be to be a medical doctor in a third world country or to be an artist. My sister is an artist, and I find her work very inspiring. And, having had the support of hospice, I sometimes think how good it would be to be a hospice nurse. But if you're asking if I regret my choices and prefer to be doing something else with my life—no. My life has been very full and very happy.

Is there anything in particular that's made you the happiest?

I think I've been enormously blessed and fortunate in the people I've met along the way. . . . The things I've done have made for a very happy, fulfilled life. When all is said and done, though, what really makes me happy and gives meaning to my life is a wonderful combination of intimacy, community and meaningful work. I have so many really good friends. Friendships like that make me happiest. Community has been significant too. I'm part of a wonderful group of women—the Sisters of St. Joseph of Baden—and a terrific faith community at St. Thomas More Parish. But community, for me, is much more inclusive and expansive. The absolute conviction that we are one human family, all of us brothers and sisters, is a great challenge and gives me great joy.

As I've struggled with cancer for the past two years, I realize how fortunate I am to have a wonderful support system. I have dear, dear friends who keep me company along the way. Although the journey is a lonely one at times, I know I do not walk alone.

Some of my happiest experiences of community are the annual backpack trips shared with university students in my campus ministry days. . . . Every spring or fall, a group of us took to the beautiful trails of Shenandoah National Park—being together, sharing together, helping one another, enjoying the beauty of the back country. Sometimes, when I feel overwhelmed with cancer and my inability to do the things I used to do, I think back to my backpacking days, pull out my old pictures, and remember. Those memories give me great joy.

Do you have any particular plans for the future?

My goal is to live fully every day that I'm given. My cancer . . . well, there's no cure for me. I've been through two complete cycles of chemotherapy, and now the cancer is active again. So my future, in terms of a healthy life, is not real great. I want to stay at the parish as long as I can. I find a lot of life there and I like to think that I give a lot of life by being there.

I think I've taken care of whatever unfinished business I may have had . . . in terms of forgiveness, resentment, hurt. I don't have the luxury—if it ever was a luxury—of being able to carry a grudge or hold on to a resentment, or to not forgive an offense.

I think that's important, for peace of mind, closures, good-byes. . . . Knowing I may not have a lot of time, I want to take care of things now, while I still can. I feel that I'm really lucky.

80

Having cancer which is fairly advanced has caused me to think about what's really important in my life, and what I want to do in the time I have left.

Do you have any advice for other people?

I don't usually give advice. But if I did, I would hope that forgiveness would be paramount. I don't know that there can ever be real happiness without forgiveness. . . .

I find myself thinking a fair bit about dying these days. Surprisingly, it isn't morbid at all. I think it's Ecclesiastes that says, "There is a time for everything." I know that I couldn't have thought so serenely about my own dying even three years ago. There is, indeed, a time for everything.

Why can you think differently about it now?

Well, for one thing, I've had two years of living with cancer. Also, my brother Bob died two and a half years ago, and my mom died last year. Both of those deaths were very significant for me. . . .

Several months ago, I participated in a workshop for persons with life-challenging diseases. One day we did a guided imagery exercise where we built a sanctuary—a place to go to find serenity. I built my sanctuary in the mountains of the Shenandoah. Toward the end of the exercise, we were instructed to invite anyone we wanted to come to our sanctuary. Without my thinking about it at all, my brother Bob came. He had died two years earlier. But he came gliding in with walking stick in hand, obviously ready for a hike. He smiled and said, "Marg, I've come to invite you to come with me." And I said, "Oh Bob, I'd really like to go with you, but I'm not ready yet." "That's okay," he said. "Whenever you're ready, I just want you to know that I'll be here for you."

It wasn't morbid at all. In fact, every time I think of it, I feel deep joy. Bob and I were great friends. I believe that, when it's time for me to die, Bob will be here for me.

I'm sure there are people who will smile condescendingly about that experience. I really don't care. I know that the memory of it gives me enormous joy and comfort. That's enough for me.

. . .

I don't know what's on the other side of death, but I believe in a God who is faithful, whose love is stronger than death. So I believe that whatever is on the other side is much more joyful than anything we can know here. Believing that, I do not fear death.

5

Having a Positive Attitude: Perseverance

The importance of having a positive attitude and persevering through difficult circumstances is illustrated by a number of the interviews. Many of the interviewees were confronted with severe hardships at various points in their lives, such as losing their parents at an early age, growing up during the Depression, facing discrimination, struggling to make ends meet, or coping with life-threatening illnesses. They did not, however, give up in the face of such setbacks, but instead worked hard to try to overcome them. And ultimately, they succeeded in leading full and satisfying lives.

FELICIA GOUDLOCK
MOUNTAIN AREA HOSPICE

I was born and raised in Asheville, North Carolina. I'm sixty-eight years old. I've lived most of my life here, except when I went off to school. I attended an all-girls' school in Concord, North Carolina for four years. I majored in business education.

My mother and father had ten children. I was the second. I only have one sister here in North Carolina now. Everybody else lives out of town. I have one sister and two brothers who live in Columbus, Ohio. I have two sisters who live in Los Angeles. I have one brother at a nursing home in North Carolina. I have a sister who lives in Monroe, North Carolina.

. . .

When I was growing up, I had to help take care of my brothers and sisters. Being the second oldest, I had to be momma number two. My mother was not what you'd call a strong person. She was kind of a "lean on" person—dependent. She was a loner. She didn't like the public. She stayed home most of the time, and just raised the children. She saw that we went to school and church. My father played a big part in helping with what he called his duties around the house, like taking care of the grass and furnace. He loved to do odds and ends around the house. He was an orderly at one of the government hospitals. He worked there for twenty-five years. He was a quiet man. He didn't socialize. Most of the time he was at home, and took care of things around the house, and saw about us children. That was the extent of his life. He passed away in 1982. And we lost our mother in November 1992.

Our family was very close. We were helpful to each other. . . . We liked each other. We wanted everybody to be successful. My parents sent every one of us to college.

. . .

I knew when I was a child what I would do when I grew up. My mother started telling us when we were about five years old, what we were going to do. Back in those days, you didn't tell your parents—they told you what they wanted you to do. And we liked that. And most of the time, we turned out the way they wanted us to.

My mother told me to teach school. She was a first grade teacher herself. But after she married and had children, she stopped working, and just raised her family. So she wanted all of us to be schoolteachers. And most of us were—all the girls, but one.

. . .

I was a teacher for forty-three years. I taught high school— tenth through twelfth. Subjects that came under business, like typing and shorthand and general business, accounting.

. . .

I like Asheville very much. It's a beautiful place, and the climate is very nice. It's more of a tourist place where people come, mostly during the summer. And then we have a lot of people who are born and raised in other places who come here to retire.

. . .

I have two daughters and two granddaughters. I kept myself at home trying to raise a family, so they could make it. And they turned out pretty good, both of them. My two daughters graduated from college.

My oldest daughter lives in Asheville. . . . My baby girl lives in Durham, North Carolina. I have two little granddaughters.

One is four years old and the other one is six. I see my grand-daughters just about every day. My husband and I provide transportation for them, taking them to school, and taking them home. We both are retired.

I met my husband because I was teaching at the school, and he came over to substitute one day. The physical ed teacher that he substituted for was sort of a friend of mine, so I met him through this regular physical ed teacher. We started dating, and a year later, we got married.

. . .

What are the things that have made you the happiest in your life?

I helped my mother and father raise the children. And I was happy about that—being able to contribute to the family finan-cially. I'm the second oldest, and as soon as I finished school, I started working. I continued to live with my mother and father, and I contributed financially to the family situation, and that en-abled my brothers and sisters to go to school too. So between me and my daddy, we sent my brothers and sisters to college.

Also, when I got my daughters married, that was a happy occasion. I felt like I didn't have to be worried any more—that they would be protected. . . .

And I enjoyed helping my mother and father with the rais-ing of the children, because we wanted to be somebody. My grandmother on my mother's side was a good old wise lady. She would give you wisdom. She had what you'd call good old horse sense. She always talked about helping yourself. Where she was living, they had a thing they called—it wasn't wel-fare—it was called charity, I think. And she said that was one thing she hoped we'd never allow ourselves to get involved in—receiving charity. She said, "Always fix it so you can help yourself, and not depend on other people." She's the one that first started us on going forward, and doing everything we could to help ourselves. And it worked out nice.

. . .

*Do you think there's any particular meaning or pur-
pose to life?*

I do. I think we were born to help people. Because that's when I'm at my happiest—when I'm doing something to help somebody. And when I'm lonely and sad is when I'm just concentrating on myself. And I'm always doing for other people, in the schools. I guess I've taught about 2,300 children—maybe more than that. And I run into a lot of students that I had, and they tell me about how my class helped them get jobs, and to make it. And that makes me feel good. I saw one lady yesterday at the doctor's office, and she said, "I know you don't remember me, but in 1950, you taught me typing. I just had to touch you, and let you know that I'm doing good, and the class I took with you helped me get a job." So that makes me feel good.

. . .

There isn't anything in my life I wish I'd done differently. I helped my mother and father until I was about twenty-six years old. Well, I was really twenty-seven when I got married. That worked out real good, because I wasn't young, and I wasn't old. I really hadn't thought about getting married, because I was never into boys and dating. I concentrated most of my time on helping the family and neighbors.

. . .

I have cancer. I found out about it about [a year and a half ago]. I had my first operation in April of 1993. I got along real good. In fact, I was in remission. But it came back. And I had another operation this past April. So this is where I find myself right now. And I pray every day for a miracle, that I will come out of all this stuff. There were five churches praying for me last year, and friends that heard about me and talked to me. So I felt like I had a miracle last year, and I'm hoping I'll have miracle number two this year. Because I would like to be around to help my grandchildren to get a little bit older.

. . .

My attitude towards life didn't change when I found out I had cancer. I felt like, what's supposed to be will be. I would think, "What did I do to contribute to this?" But I can't think of anything that caused this to happen to me. And I never asked God, "Why?" I never questioned Him about why this had to happen to me, because I'm no different from anybody else. And it could happen to me like it could happen to anybody else. So I just kept a good positive attitude. I said, "I'm going to do everything the doctors tell me, and try to purify my body, and see if I can bring this to a remission." . . . So what is helping me most of all is my attitude. I said, "I'm not going to get sad and blue, or discouraged, and just give up. I'm not going to do that. I'm going to fight it and hope for the best." . . . Even though this is the second operation, I still haven't changed my mind about being hopeful. Because when you lose hope, you've lost it all. You got to keep hope.

Do you have any advice for other people about how they should live their lives?

Yes. Put God first. First of all, you have to believe in God. I learned this real early in life. Put all your faith in Jesus Christ, and everything will work out all right, whether you think so or not. And what happens, I think, is meant to be—whether it's good or bad. But there's a whole lot we can do to help ourselves. The only advice I can give to anybody is to trust God, believe in Jesus Christ, and be as Christ-like as you can.

I guess that's number one on my agenda. Number two would be education. Get all the education you can, because education is knowledge. And the more education you have, you can deal with most any situation.

And number three would be good associates. Associate with people who are uplifting, and who see life as a good thing—as a gift. So I think those would be the top three on my agenda. . . .

I think I've had a pretty good life. We're doing fine now. My husband's retired, and I'm retired, and we just do the basic, essential things of life every day. My husband takes care of me real good. He's a good cook. He feeds me, and he does the laundry and housecleaning. He is very, very good to me.

. . .

My family did overcome all the obstacles that were in our way. We had a much better life than we thought we would. We made it—my family made it real good. We did get over all the bad stuff that was blocking us, and holding us down. It came from hard work and dedication, being close and loving, and helping each other. And staying out of trouble, and taking care of family and all of that. And encouraging everybody every day to keep on doing good.

LUCILLE NOLAN
McKENZIE-WILLAMETTE HOSPICE

I'm eighty-five years old. I live in Eugene, Oregon. I was born in a small town in Pennsylvania. My father and his brother had a general store together. I don't know what happened— whether the business wasn't going so well—but we moved to Youngstown, Ohio. My father was the manager of an electrical appliance store which had outlets in other cities. He was transferred to Toledo and Dayton, and then back to Youngstown. He somehow developed something wrong with his lungs and died in 1922, at age forty-nine. My mother lived a little over a year longer, and she died of TB, when I was just a month from being fourteen.

My oldest brother was around twenty at the time. We got an apartment and lived together until he got married. My sister and I lived with him and his wife until I got married in 1927. . . .

I had six children. The first one died at a year and a half. The other five are still living. I have twenty-five grandchildren and ten great-grands. One of my children is a Catholic nun. She belongs to a community in Ohio.

I started having health problems in 1985. I went in for bypass surgery in 1986, and it was then that they discovered something wrong with my blood. It turned out to be lymphoma. Since then it's been sort of up and down. I was on medication that put me in remission for two years, and then it came back. And then in 1993, I got some terrible infection that put me in the hospital for almost two months. When I came out, I couldn't live by myself anymore—I had been living alone since 1966, when my youngest daughter married. That's when I had to sell my mobile home and my car, and my youngest daughter here in Oregon brought me out here to be with her. That was in October of 1993.

· · ·

When I was growing up, I really didn't have any idea what I would do when I became an adult. . . .

I got married when I was eighteen. I met my husband at a dance hall. It was at an amusement park. They had a beautiful ballroom there, and that's where I met him. . . . He was a very nice looking young man. He treated me very well. Maybe if my parents had lived, I wouldn't have gotten married so young. I don't know—it's hard to remember how I felt way back then.

. . .

I had left high school to start working. I worked in a five and ten, and restaurants, and things like that. I don't think I really liked it. It was something I had to do. . . .

After I got married, the only time I worked was after my first child died. After the 1929 stock market crash, my husband was out of work, so I got a job in a candy store. . . .

My first child was born in 1928, and then I didn't have any until 1933. At that time, my husband was back working in the mill, so we were able to start up housekeeping again.

During the Depression, we didn't have it as bad as many people, because my husband's father was a policeman, so he had a job. And he had two sisters living at home who were teachers, so they were in pretty good financial shape, so we stayed with them.

You must have had a pretty rough time, having your parents die, and having your first child die.

Yes, I think I probably wouldn't have gotten married so young [if my parents hadn't died]. And then I went through some pretty rough times after I got married, because my husband loved horses. He had a riding stable, and where we lived was always convenient for that. Almost twenty years of my married life were in terrible housing—sometimes with no conveniences whatsoever. So it wasn't an easy life.

But I just accepted it. I had to go on. I had the kids, and I had no parents. If I had wanted to leave, I had nowhere to go. So I stuck with it.

. . .

What are the things that have made you the happiest in your life?

I was always happy when each of the children was born healthy. Another happy time was, after my husband died, I managed to get into a house with all the conveniences—I felt like we were in the Ritz. . . .

I was supporting myself then. I went to work. . . . I did housework, I worked in restaurants, whatever I could do.

I was forty-five when my husband died; he was forty-seven.

. . .

Do you think there's any particular meaning or purpose to life?

Oh, of course. I'm a believer. One thing I started to do was to tithe whatever money I got, and not to have my wants taken care of, but my needs. And it worked out. I always was able to pay my bills. I never had to ask for any help. Everything worked out pretty good.

I'm a Catholic. My parents were Methodist, but after we moved to Ohio, they didn't go to church.

How did you get involved in the Catholic faith?

Well, I married a Catholic, but that wasn't the reason I became Catholic—it was something that I read that just struck me. It's the part in the Bible where Jesus said to Peter—the word "Peter" means "rock," or it did at that time—"Thou art Peter, and upon this rock I will build my church. And the gates of hell will never prevail against it."

. . .

I believe there's a heaven and a hell.

What do you think heaven is like?

That's one thing I've been wondering about. I just wonder—will I meet my parents, and my little son who died? It's fantastic—I can't imagine what it will be like. But it will be good.

Is there anything in your life that you wish you'd done differently?

Probably I shouldn't have married so young. But we all make mistakes. I don't think I made any major mistakes. I just go with what I did, and presume it was okay.

. . .

You're going to laugh, but one thing I miss is ballroom dancing. My husband and I used to go dancing quite a lot. In fact, when I was a kid, I wanted to take dancing lessons. I never did get to do that. When I was a kid, I felt a little cheated that I didn't get to take dancing lessons. I wanted to tap dance—oh, that's great! [Laughs.]

. . .

I learned about the lymphoma on the phone. The doctor called me and told me I had it—I don't think that was the proper way to inform me. I just wondered, "How did I get this? What happened? Why?" Then I kept getting blood every month. It's been a pretty rough thing, but there's lots of worse things that could happen. . . .

I don't think my attitude towards life has changed. I try to be optimistic. When you read the papers and hear about all these horrible things that are going on, you feel pretty blessed with whatever you have.

. . .

Do you have any advice for other people about how they should live their lives?

Well, I hope they all have some beliefs of some kind in a higher being, whatever their faith is. And just try to treat other people as you would have them treat you.

Do you have any particular plans for the future?

[Laughs.] I don't know if I have one. All I can do is just take each day as it comes, and be glad for it. I read about people who are blind, and I think, "Oh, thank God I can see." My hearing isn't so good, but that's all right—I have a hearing aid. I'm just as happy as I can be under the circumstances. I just thank God that I've had this little extra time. How long that will be, I don't know.

ANNA KRAUSE
ALLEGHENY HOSPICE

I grew up in a very small suburban town, right outside Pittsburgh. I'm eighty-three years old. I come from a family with five boys and five girls. I was the first girl, after four boys. . . . I lost a son with cancer. He had leukemia. He died when he was twenty years old. . . . I have two sons living. And I have four grandchildren—two boys and two girls.

I worked most of my life. In those days, we had it very hard. I grew up when people really had nothing. They had their own gardens and everything. We had our own very large garden, plus two hundred chickens. So that's how my mother kept us all going.

At that time, you did what your parents told you to do. You weren't allowed to talk back to them or anything, or your fa-

95

ther would give you the dirty looks, and you knew what that meant. I'll never forget the time I told my mother, "Oh, I don't feel like going to church today." She said to me, "You walk in your brothers' footsteps." There was a lot of snow. I went to church, I'll tell you.

There was no telling them that you wanted to stay in bed or had a headache. When I told my mother I didn't want to go to school, I had a headache, she'd say, "You go to school and you'll feel better." And I did.

In those days, you didn't need a working permit. You just went to work when you were sixteen. And that's what I did. I went to downtown Pittsburgh here, and I got a job in a room where they would mark the clothes. And I just went there, for this big department store, and I worked myself up. [After that], I went to work for the H.J. Heinz Company, because they gave you good money. But you had all odd hours. If they told you to work night turn, you worked night turn. And that's what I did.

I did all kinds of work for them. I made ketchup pouches, I worked in the can room. You were on the line, whatever they did. I finally put in to be a scale girl, to weigh the ketchup pouches. And I liked that. It was fast work, and you got paid by the hour. But boy, I worked, I tell you. . . .

I met my husband at a party when I was nineteen. . . . I was twenty-two when I got married. I didn't have any children for five years. . . . My husband and I were married for thirty years.

I lost my husband. When the Second World War broke out, I had the three boys. They were all Air Force boys. My husband was in the Navy. I was stuck then with two little ones, and one thirteen month old. And as they grew up, they all volunteered for the Air Force.

And then when the oldest boy got out of the Air Force, I just had him with me for eighteen months. He had cancer, and I lost him. But oh, did he suffer. He really suffered. He couldn't even stand a sheet or anything touching him. And if he would reach for a glass of water, he was like in a spasm. . . .

After I lost him, it brought me closer to church. After that, I helped out at all the church dinners, had a rummage room in the church for seven years and helped out other people. We're very close in our church. I know, since I've been laid up, how good the people have been to me.

. . .

When I was growing up, I didn't have anything in mind that I would do when I became an adult. Only my brother, who turned out to be a minister, had a college education. My parents didn't have that kind of money.

. . .

What are the things that have made you the happiest in your life?

Well, I play the organ. I do crafts. I keep in touch with the people that I know that aren't in church. I haven't been in church since last October. I haven't been able to make it. I have to get on a bus to go to church, and I haven't been able to walk it. . . . I have an awful lot of friends, too. And I keep myself busy, letter-writing.

. . .

Do you think there's any particular meaning or purpose to life?

Oh yes, there's a meaning to life. God wants all of us to change our ways, that's for sure.

Is there anything in your life that you wish you'd done differently?

There was one time, after I lost my husband, that I was thinking about becoming a nurse. What changed my mind was,

97

at that time, [my son] was only fifteen, going to school. Where would he be after school? And I thought of those things, and I thought, "No, I do not want him coming home to an empty house." I said, "No, that's no good for him." And I'm glad I did.

When my kids were small, they stuck together. They still stick together. When you called one of them, you knew the other two were right with him. You knew they stuck together. And they're still very close.

. . .

[Ms. Krause discussed her cancer, which was first diagnosed approximately fourteen years earlier. She was treated with chemotherapy for four months and was admitted to the hospital.]

Well, I stayed in the hospital for three weeks and I was no better. One day, I told the doctor, "Doctor, I'm giving up the treatments." The doctor said, "There's no use giving up the treatments, because the treatments and the medicine go to-gether." I said, "All right then, I'm giving those up." Do you know that, after that, I had ten good years? They couldn't get over it. . . . [But] three years ago, it came back.

. . .

Do you have any explanation for why you got better the first time?

I put my faith in the Lord. I thought, "If anybody's going to make me well, it's going to be Him." And right now, they can't get over how good I'm getting along again. Because I've been sick this time. . . . I really had no summer at all last year. I couldn't go anywhere or do anything.

But now, I'm getting better again. The other day, I went up the street three blocks.

. . .

Did your attitude towards life change at all when you learned you had cancer?

Well, it does. It makes you think. And the first thing you think is, "Why me? How did I get cancer?"

Do you have any advice for other people about how they should live their lives?

The first thing is, if you have a family, try to bring your children up right. Talk with them. Don't scold them. Don't hit them. You can punish them. You can take something from them that they like most. And you can tell them they're grounded. These teenagers would be a lot different if they had listened to their parents. But parents nowdays are getting weaker and weaker with their children. They don't talk to them enough. They don't have time for them. They don't care where they go, as long as they don't have to bother with them.

When mine were growing up, I always told them, "If you have any problems, you come to me. We will sit down, we will talk it over. We will see what we can do." My husband was quick-tempered, and he didn't have patience with them. I've got a lot of patience. And we would talk it over.

And when they were in high school, I said to them, "You invite your little girlfriends. They can come home with you. I want to meet whoever you're with. We have games you can play. We can put the badminton out in the yard. We can give them a soft drink or cookie or something." I always did a lot of baking. I said, "You can have all the fun you want, but you're off of the streets. You're not chasing around."

And if you take it all the way through life with your children, they think the world of you. I know mine do.

. . .

The other night, they had this program on tv about donating your organs. And I was thinking, "I wonder if I should do that?" To give somebody else life. Only I'm so old, they may not want them. [Laughs.]

It sounds like you're still doing well though.

Oh, I am. I'm doing wonderful.

かん

BERTRAND FONTAINE
CLOVER HOSPICE

I grew up in the state of Maine, in the Lewiston-Auburn area. I'm sixty-five years old. With the exception of three years when I lived in Idaho, I spent all my time working here in the state of Maine, raising my family. . . . I had two brothers and a sister. One brother is deceased.

I have good memories of my childhood. We never were in hardship, lacking for food or clothes. We weren't rich, but we had a car, and not every family had a car in those days. We were never hungry. I'd say we were comfortable—lower-to-middle, I guess they'd call it now.

I liked living in this area. I didn't know anything different. But knowing what I know now, I still like it. I'm not a big city character. I guess I wasn't around certain things, so you don't miss what you don't have.

As I grew older and got married, I went into business for myself—I got a neighborhood grocery store. It's nothing that you'd get rich on, but we had a similar situation when I was young. We had plenty to eat, and there was no problems. Plenty of work, but plenty to eat too.

One thing I did know, I didn't want my children to go that

way—I wanted better for them. I think most of us in those times, it's natural for parents to want better for their kids than they had for themselves. Not that it was bad, but you want better.

. . .

I got married when I was eighteen. I met my wife towards the end of the Second World War. It was either VJ-Day or VE-Day, whichever one occurred first. The town had a celebration. They closed a couple streets for playing music and a celebration and dancing. There were two or three days of revelry— celebrating the end of the War. I think I met my wife during that time. We went out together for two years before we got married.

My father had a small grocery store. That's how I happened to know that end of the business. He would have liked me to follow in his footsteps. So I had my choice of that, and then I was married. Then I had to decide if I should go to school. I knew I could do better if I went to school. I was interested in accounting, or in that field. It's just decisions we have to make in life. And I decided that I would be satisfied in wanting this life. And I'm not sorry.

. . .

I have four boys; three of them are engineers and one's an electrician. The two oldest went to college in Massachusetts. . . . My third son got a technical degree, and he's an electrician. My youngest son is an engineer, too. . . . Two of my sons are in Virginia, one's in New Hampshire and one is in Maine. . . .

My wife passed away three years ago. . . .

I have twelve grandchildren. I'm very fortunate. The family, even though we're kind of far apart in miles, we're a very close family. And seeing the condition I've been in, they've kind of exerted themselves to come up quite often.

I have one son who's here locally. I still have my home, and he goes there and cuts the grass and takes care of the snow. My other two, when they come from out of town, they got a place to stay. It's a close family, and I feel it's really, really helped me a lot.

. . .

I got into the grocery business because I was aware of it, and knew of it. I never had my father's store. I had gone out west and tried that. When you're young, you try to make more money. And I had gone to Idaho. My brother was in the service, and had gotten married and lived out there. And the money was better out there than here. So I went out there, and we lived there for three years. But my wife was very homesick. The culture was very different. So we decided to come back. We knew it would be less money, but that we'd still make a living, and we did. That's how I happened to get back into groceries, because it was something I knew. I had an opportunity to get in with very little money, so that's how I got started. I owned the store for sixteen years, I think.

It was a lot of work. There's a certain amount of sacrifice. I didn't want my wife to work with me steady, in the store. I wanted her with the children. She helped me in a lot of ways, and the kids helped me in the store. And I had one full-time clerk, which is about as small as you can get, I guess. It's one of those things where I made a living. It was hard work, long hours. But I think we had a happy life. I'd like to think so, and everything I've heard is that it appears to be.

I eventually sold the store. Liquidation would be the best word—there wasn't much there to sell, really.

From there I went to work for a wholesale house. It's a wholesale house I used to buy from. They were in groceries, and then they had a division with tobacco, candy, health and beauty aids—things like that. I went to work for them in the health and beauty aid section, and candy. I was familiar with it, because I had worked in the retail end. . . .

Eventually, I retired from that. I was starting to have a hard time handling the work. It came to a time with the age, and the family was growing up, that I decided it was time to move on. After I had retired for a little while, I wanted to find something that was less demanding. So I worked for a program they had for people out of work around my age. It wasn't strenuous. It was light desk work. It was at the courthouse. I did that for two or three years. Then after that, I went to work as a full employee at a local bank.

. . .

Is there anything in particular that's made you the happiest in your life?

My life as a whole was quite fulfilled. With my family, and what the children have accomplished. We just took our enjoyment out of family living, I'd say. I never made a big achievement that made me real happy. . . . It might sound kind of dull, but I was satisfied with that.

Do you think there's any particular meaning or purpose to life?

There certainly is. I certainly feel that we're here on earth to fulfill a purpose, and our just reward will be when we meet our Maker and see how He likes what we've done. . . .

I won't say I'm religious. I believe in all of it, and I feel that I'm doing as well as I am because of people praying for me. And I've had wonderful people praying hard. I don't claim that I'm a religious person—I don't think I am. But I do believe in all these things.

Is there anything in your life that you wish you'd done differently?

Well, there's a lot of little things, but not any big things. You go back and examine, and wish you'd had a little more education or gone into this field a little bit more. But who knows how it would have turned out? Really, I don't know how to answer that.

. . .

I have lymphoma. I first learned about it eight and a half years ago. And at the time, they felt that if they could check it, and no signs of it came back within five years, that you were cured. It went away for over five years, but then it cropped up again, and then it didn't stop. I had a lot of treatment— chemotherapy, radiation therapy, surgery. But I always was able to bounce back. I was very, very fortunate.

Did your attitude towards life change when you found out you had lymphoma?

Of course it affects you. But I had a lot of support—it just is unbelievable—from people I didn't know, to friends and family. I just had a lot of support. Even though it affected me, I think I took it well enough. You change what you can, and what you can't change, you try to live with as well as you can.

Do you have any advice for other people about how they should live their lives?

I never felt that I should give advice to anybody else. It's a one day at a time thing. Keep your ears open, and your eyes open, and try to learn from life around you, and I think you'll improve your own.

How did you like living in Idaho?

I liked it. It was mountainous, with very small communities. My brother lived there—that's the reason we went to that particular community. I liked it. . . . If it wouldn't have been for my wife being as lonely, maybe we would have stayed there a little longer. Who knows about life? The decisions we make all our life, one day at a time, can turn our whole life around.

ॐ

MARGARET DOWNEY
VNA HOSPICE

I was born in Pennsylvania, many years ago. I grew up in small towns and in the country. When I was in my last year of high school, we moved to Steubenville, Ohio, and I went to school there and graduated. . . . I have three brothers and three sisters.

My dad was a farmer and a miner and a handyman, and stuff like that. Then we finally moved to Cleveland—my dad got injured and he couldn't do a lot of things, so he came out here and did custodian work. And we all ended up here in Cleveland.

. . .

I've thought about moving away from Cleveland, but I'm so old now, and I have my home paid for, and I have a couple of my children that stay with me, so I'm not alone. I have two sons in Georgia and four children around here. I've thought of [moving], but then I thought, "Gee, where else could I have a whole home, and just pay taxes and utilities?" So I'm staying.

The neighborhood isn't the best anymore. I've been in this home for thirty years now, and it isn't the best, but it's fine with me. I have a nice yard, and a nice garage, and I enjoy it.

. . .

The first time I got married, I was twenty-two. The way I met my husband was, my mother took in people who she would cook for. They'd eat their meals there, and she'd pack their lunches. And my brother and my father at the time worked at the same place that they did. They had their own home, but they ate with us. My first husband was the son of one of those men. I met him through his father. We lived in New Jersey after we got married. But we divorced after nine years. I had three children, and we divorced.

I got remarried in 1955. After I remarried, I had three more children, so I have a large family also. . . . My youngest child will be thirty-five in about a month. I have a child that's going to be forty-seven, and the rest are in between.

My second husband and I both worked at the same grocery store. He was a stocker, and I was a cashier. We moved here to Cleveland in 1943, and I've been here ever since. My husband worked in the steel mill for thirty-six years. He's deceased now. He died three years ago. He was from Kentucky, but this was where the work was, so this is where we stayed. . . .

I worked between children, and I worked when he'd be laid off or something down at the mill. I worked up until 1978. I fell in 1977 and hurt myself. I tried working, but I just couldn't manage it, so I haven't worked since 1978.

I just had my birthday last week—I'm seventy. Well, I think it's a good thing—I'm still walking around.

. . .

Is there anything in your life that's made you the happiest?

I don't know—I've done so many things, and had such a good life. I really don't know. I went to the Marine Corps Ball once. That was very nice. My son was a Marine. . . . I've had three of my sons in the service. That was nice. And then we've made trips.

I think the thing that made me the happiest is the fact that I finally learned to drive, and could go when I wanted to. I didn't learn to drive until 1950. I enjoy going every place, taking the children out on picnics. I've gone to Florida to see one of my children, and to Pennsylvania. I just think that was a great thing.

. . .

Are there any particular times in your life that stand out?

Well, I was proud of the fact that I graduated. I thought that was nice. I don't know—I used to complain constantly because we lived in the country, on the farm. It seemed like you never had a minute to say, "Well, I don't have anything to do." But now that I'm not on the farm, I think it would be wonderful to be back.

I miss just being able to be out. Here, I'm afraid to even go out. Just being able to go out. I had a good life. I grew up, and I was happy. I had a good life.

And when I tell these children about having to keep the coal stoves going, and carry water up from the stream, they think, "Grandma, you are so silly." They think I'm telling them a lot of stories that aren't true.

At the time, I thought it was terrible, but now I see I was happy, because I really enjoyed it.

The kind of work we did on the farm was just what kids generally do. Like every week, you'd clean the house, and watch the little ones, and help with the cooking. You'd do things, you'd do chores. It's not like the kids now—every time they do something they say, "Well, what do I get for it?" You did chores. That's part of growing up.

. . .

107

*Do you think there's any particular meaning or pur-
pose to life?*

Well, I don't know, but if there isn't, I'm sure wasting a lot
of my time. And everybody else is too.

I think it's important that you enjoy what you're doing.
And I know the grandkids, they think I'm pretty silly, but they
all love me. And I'm pretty proud of the fact that, one day
when I was saying something, one of the grandkids said to the
other, "Don't you do that, because grandma said, 'No,' and if
she said no, that's it." And then another one was telling me a
lie, and I knew it was a lie, and the other one spoke up and
said, "Grandma does not lie, and don't you lie to grandma."
And that's the thing I impress on them the most—don't tell a
lie. Tell the truth, even if it gets you in trouble. You'll be in
more trouble when you're found out. I have them around all
the time.

The oldest grandchild is twenty-three. And then I have a
grandchild that's seventeen, sixteen, fifteen, fourteen, thirteen
and eleven. They kind of go all in a group there.

. . .

*Is there anything in your life that you wish you'd done
differently?*

I think the best thing I could have done differently—and I
still could, but I probably never will—is stop being so determined, and stubborn and bossy. One of my boys told me the
other day, "Boy mom, you are determined, aren't you?" And I
said, "Oh yes, I am." I just always tried, when I do something,
do it right.

That's what made my son say, "Mom, you're determined."
He's never had to do a lot of things, and now he does them
for me here. He doesn't do them exactly the way I think they
ought to be done, and I'll go in back of him and say, "Nope,

you missed that spot. Nope, you don't do it that way." And he just doesn't care for that.

. . .

I have two sons who are staying with me here now, because they don't want me to be alone. They drive me anyplace I want to go. And they call me throughout the day to make sure that I'm okay, because I've fallen a lot, and they're always worried. I'm not usually alone, but when I am, they keep checking on me. Every time they go out, they leave a telephone number where they can be reached, in case they're needed. So they take good care of me.

. . .

I have a liver illness—cirrhosis—and it's a terminal case. I've been sick off and on, and I've had a lot of illness, but last September I passed out, and they put me in the hospital. That's when they told me they didn't think that I would pull through. They didn't think they'd see me coming home. And I told them I was coming back. So I came home eleven days later, and for two weeks, I couldn't get up or down by myself. And a therapist was coming out, and home nursing care, and Meals on Wheels, and when the therapist came out, he said, "Well, I don't know if you're going to get up and walk." And I said, "You want to bet?" And two weeks later, he came out and said, "You don't need me anymore." I told him I was going to walk, and I did.

. . .

They told me that I'm in remission at the present time. That it will never get better, but I can go for a while with it not getting any worse. They keep telling me, "Well, you know you're terminal." And I tell them, "I know, but I'm living while I'm alive, and the heck with that." . . .

My attitude towards life hasn't really changed since I got sick, because everybody has something that's going to happen to them sooner or later. I'm just lucky. Like I say, I'm lucky I made that birthday. I was looking forward to reaching the seventy mark. Because they told me I wouldn't. First, it was, "Well, let's get through Thanksgiving." Then Christmas. And then my birthday next, and I got through that too. So I just showed 'em I could do it.

Do you have any goals or plans for the future?

Oh, I have plans. The plans I have are work. I love working in my yard. The weeds are about as high as my waist, and I haven't had a chance . . . . The weather isn't the best around here, and I haven't had a chance, but I told 'em, "Boy, just wait until I can get outside." That I like. And I haven't done that lately.

. . .

Do you have any advice for other people about how they should live their lives?

Well, I found out a long time ago that it doesn't do you any good to try to tell anybody anything. You just go along with what they're doing, and if you think it will help, you help them. . . . I want [my kids] to be all right. I worry when they take the car, and hope they don't get hurt. Things like that, like all parents do. But I don't try to tell them what to do. There's just no sense in that. They're hardheaded like their mother anyway.

There's a lot of times that I've helped people, or tried. To some people around this neighborhood, I'm Mrs. D; to everybody else, I'm either mom or grandma. That's because the grandkids are around a lot. There's very few people that ever call me Mrs. Downey. I'm not even sure half of 'em know my name is Downey. But I'm just ma or grandma all the time. And the kids know that if mom isn't home, you can go to Mrs.

Downey's, and she'll have you come in and wait until they get there. And they've always been told that if they're in any kind of trouble, or need anything, just go to Mrs. Downey's, and she'll help you. So this is the gathering place for young children whenever they need anything.

There have been some who have moved out of the neighborhood who come by every now and then just to say hello. And I've got kids here who are grown now and have their own kids, who have been coming around here for the last thirty years, and they still stop in just to say, "Hi, how are you?" So they're pretty nice kids.

. . .

I don't let things bother me. If I get 'em done, fine. If I don't, they'll be there tomorrow, or the next day or maybe forever. But I like to keep busy. I hate not doing anything. . . . I haven't ventured out yet to drive or take long walks, or anything like that, but I do keep active.

. . .

There's nothing else I think I can tell you. Except I'm old and ugly.

. . .

It's been a good life as far as I'm concerned. I have healthy children. I have all my children around. I think it's a very good thing. I think we just had a real nice family.

MILDRED STONE
FAMILY HOME HOSPICE

I'm seventy-six years old. I was born in Burlington, Kansas. I graduated from high school in Burlington. I've worked for the public ever since I was fourteen. I lived in Burlington until the start of the war. Then I married a military man and moved around over the country, and lived in various places.

I had one brother—he's deceased. Then I have a sister somewhere—I don't know where she is.

. . .

I liked Burlington all right—until I found out there were other places. [Laughs.] . . . After I left Burlington and got to moving around, I found out that there were a lot of pretty places. One of my favorites was Monterey, California. I lived in Monterey for about fifteen years. Both of my boys graduated from Monterey High School. I worked for the Board of Education as a cost accountant for the transportation department. I worked there for about twelve and a half years.

. . .

I have two sons. One is living in Texas and the other is a deputy sheriff in Wyoming. So they're kind of scattered out. . . . I've got three grandsons and a granddaughter. And then I've got a great-grandson—he'll be two next October.

. . .

When I was fourteen, I worked for a tea parlor—a luncheon tea room. And they also made candy. After that I went to work in a bakery. And then after graduating from high school, I went to work for [a variety store], and I was there until 1940, when I got married.

I worked my way through high school by working at the bakery—I worked from 3:00 to 10:00 each night.

. . .

Was it hard for you to work your way through high school?

Oh, I probably didn't make as good a grades as I would have if I hadn't had to work. But that was during the Depression, and I had a father who believed that a girl could learn all she needed to know after the eighth grade from her mother.

He had sent my brother, and my brother had a car, and he had band instruments. So when I graduated from eighth grade, I told my mother, "Well, I want to go to high school." She was behind me. In Kansas, you have to buy your own supplies, so I just worked and saved my money, and I put myself through high school.

My brother, who my dad gave everything he wanted, never did graduate from high school. But I graduated.

My mother came to visit me one time, and while she was visiting, I made her a new dress. Of course, my dad always noticed when she had a new dress or a new hairdo. He met her at the train when she got home and said, "Oh, you got a new dress!" And she said, "Yeah, Mildred made it for me." He said, "Mildred! Where'd she learn to sew?" And mom said, "In high school."

She never let him forget that he made it easy for my brother, but didn't do a damn thing for me in going to high school, and I was the one that got the diploma. She rubbed that in to him every time she could. And he'd say, "Yeah, I know, I know." He got to feel pretty bad about it.

But really, I don't think it hurt me. I think it was good for me. I think that's half of what's the matter with so many kids today, is they have everything given to them. They don't know the value of a dollar. They're bored to death, and they get in trouble.

. . .

Now don't misunderstand me—my dad was a good father. And he loved me—the way we'd get together and sing his old songs, and argue politics. If I took the part of a Democrat, he was the best Republican you ever heard, and vice versa. He just didn't believe that a girl needed to go to high school. But he changed his mind after he found out what I could do.

But I think it was good for me. I don't hold any grudges at all.

. . .

I met my first husband at a dance in Burlington. He was from Waverly, which was about fifteen miles from Burlington.

Was it love at first sight?

No, no, no, no. I just can't make up my mind that fast. I got to mull things over for a while.

I was sixteen when I met him. Married him when I was twenty-two. My dad thought I never was going to get married. A lot of the girls at my time in high school got engaged during graduation, and were married afterwards. But I stayed single and worked. But I figured, when you got married, you were married for a heck of a long time.

. . .

My first husband and I divorced in 1962. I remarried in 1967.

. . .

My second husband and I met in Monterey, and we moved up to Klamath Falls, Oregon. . . . We lived up there for about fifteen years. Previous to my meeting him, he had lived in the desert, and he liked it. So he wanted to come back to the desert. But his idea of coming down to the desert was to get five acres out in the boonies. And I said, "No way. As old as we are, I don't think that's the thing. And I am scared to death of snakes and lizards and what have you. And you know, I would have to stay in the house if we lived out like that. And if anything happened to you, I'd sure have to move." So I said, "If you want to live in the desert, we'll have to live in town. And besides, when you get that old, you shouldn't be too far away from the doctor and the hospital." So that's why we moved to Las Vegas.

· · ·

What are the things that have made you the happiest in your life?

Working, I think. I was one that, I don't care what I was doing, I enjoyed it. Now I had jobs that I liked better than others, but I liked every one I had. . . .

You won't believe this, but it's been about twenty-four years since I left the Monterey Board of Education. But I really, really liked it. It was interesting. And do you know, to this day, I often dream that I'm back doing that work. So you see it made an impression on me.

· · ·

Do you think there's any particular meaning or purpose to life?

Well, I think you live the best life that you can live. The cleanest, most thoughtful, considerate life that you can live.

· · ·

There's nothing in my life I wish I'd done differently. I just wish I knew I could live longer—that's all. I have no regrets—I've had a pretty good life. I had two boys—they never gave

115

me a minute of trouble. Of course, I spent time with them. When they were growing up, they were my main objective.

. . .

I have lung disease—asthma, chronic asthma.

They signed me over to hospice in November of 1991. They told my husband I was going to die. So my husband said, "Well, if she's going to die, I want to take her home, where she can be around familiar things." I don't think he knew what he was getting into, saying he was going to take care of me. But by George, he brought me home and took care of me. Of course, hospice backed him up. He hand-fed me, and he bathed me, and changed my bed and did the laundry—he did everything.

And by golly, I just got stubborn and said, "I'm not gonna die." And I'm still here.

. . .

I was flat on my back in bed from November 1991 to July 1992. I'd been in bed so long, I had forgotten how to turn over. I had to learn all that. They had the therapist come down and teach me how to walk.

. . .

Right now, I feel all right, as long as I'm sitting or laying down. But the least bit of energy or excitement, and I have trouble breathing. I'm on oxygen twenty-four hours a day. But I just cannot exert myself.

. . .

I don't think my attitude towards life has changed at all. Like I tell you, I have no regrets. I think when you come that close to dying, if you have any regrets, that's when they come forward.

I would hate to leave my husband, because my second husband is a jewel. And I hate to leave my boys.

. . .

Do you have any advice for other people about how they should live their lives?

I think they should live it as full as they can, with some regard for living it right. Now I'm not what you'd call a religious fanatic, but I do believe you reap what you sow. And if you live right, you'll enjoy life a lot more than if you try to get around and do everybody dirty.

I don't know . . . I'm a happy person.

❧

6

Consideration for Others

When asked whether they had any advice about how life should be lived, many of the interviewees said we should be more considerate of others. Indeed, a number of the interviewees (particularly those in their sixties or older) remarked on what they perceived as an unraveling of the fabric of our society, as reflected by increasing violence, a rising divorce rate, and a decline in the traditional family unit. Many said they believed people needed to make a greater effort to get along with each other and treat one another fairly. Perhaps the knowledge of one's own impending demise makes it clearer that we are all in the same position—we are all vulnerable, fallible creatures who share many of the same needs and desires—and that it is more important to try to live in peace with our neighbors than to try to get ahead of them.

LAUREL SNOOK
ARBOR HOSPICE

I grew up in western Iowa. I live now in Ypsilanti, Michigan. I'm eighty-nine years old. We've been here in Michigan for fifty-two years now. I've got nine brothers and sisters. They're not all living, but there was ten of us. I'm the oldest. . . . There's five of us that have already died with cancer. It just seems to run right down the line. There were five boys and five girls. Until about twenty-five years ago—then they started having cancer one by one.

. . .

The reason we came [to Michigan] is that my daughter had dust asthma. You're not old enough, I don't suppose, to remember the great dust storms they had back in the 1930's. And her asthma got so bad, we had to go someplace, so we came here and it helped her.

. . .

The rest of my family is scattered everywhere. I've got two in California, one in Des Moines, Iowa, one in Promise City, Iowa, and I'm here. We just got scattered out as we got older, got married and had different jobs.

I started out as a teacher when I was eighteen, and then I became a Bible teacher. I did that for fifty-some years. I did that until January of this year, when my cancer got so bad that I couldn't get around anymore, and I had to quit. . . . I always liked to teach. During the Depression, I taught public schools for three and a half years. And then we came to Michigan, and I found out the best thing here was to get in the shops. I worked for Ford Motor Company most all the time, until I retired at sixty-two. But teaching was always my first love.

. . .

My father was a farmer for many years. But he worked for the state and the federal government the last eighteen or twenty years. I never really considered going into farming myself. I never cared much for farming after . . . . You're not old enough to remember, but after the Great Depression come in 1934, farming has never come back.

. . .

My family's farm had livestock, and soybeans and corn. We raised soybean and corn for feed, but we raised hogs and cattle mostly. All the kids had to do chores around the farm. I don't think I minded that so bad. I've always tried to adjust myself to whatever I'm doing. You'll find out that, if you try to adjust yourself to what you're doing, you'll get along a lot better.

. . .

The Depression was a bad time. Both of our parents were pretty well off when all the banks went broke in the Midwest, and they lost everything they had. I was about twenty-nine then. And everything went bad. Seventy percent of the farmers in Iowa, and the businesses too, were in bad shape for several years.

I went to teaching after farming got so bad. Teaching was better than lots of other things. And then teaching got bad because young married girls would try to get a school close to their home, and they got down so they was teaching for twenty-five dollars a month. There was no sense in a married man trying to work for that. My father was acquainted with some people in the highway commission, and I worked for the highway commission for several years. So I've had a rather diversified life. But I enjoyed it. I enjoyed every minute of it. I've always been a person who tried to adjust myself to whatever I was in.

. . .

My wife and I were high school sweethearts. We were going together when she was in the tenth grade, and I was in the eleventh grade. We got married when we were both twenty. We've been married sixty-nine years this fall. So we've had quite a life together. . . .

I knew back in the eleventh grade in high school that she was the one I wanted to marry. We never changed our minds.

We were both basketball players. That's how we got started. She played on the girls' team and I played on the boys' team. . . .

I don't know if there's any secret to having a good marriage. You've got to see the other person's point—both sides have got to live. We like the same things, and we got along very well. We went to church together, and worked at church together. I taught Bible class in the church for forty-five years, and she taught youngsters about that long. Then we got working with young people—young teens and people in their early twenties. We did that for many years. I suppose that was our life calling as much as anything, because we enjoyed it. We still enjoy it.

We've done everything together. When I retired, we traveled for three years. We've seen forty-four of the lower forty-eight [states]. We've seen two provinces in Canada, and we were in Mexico. I never was in Alaska. I was satisfied with this, I guess.

I enjoyed it every step of the way. I don't enjoy the cancer that I have now. But cancer runs strong in our family. We have to accept it and make the best of it. Because the Lord's been so good to us in so many ways, we couldn't object to it.

I don't like cancer—it's a terrible thing. It took about sixty or seventy pounds off of me in about six months now. And there's no way of stopping it. The doctors say the cancer's just eating my body up. But it's been a good life, and I wouldn't want to complain too much.

123

*What are the things that have made you the happiest
in your life?*

Probably Bible teaching—that probably would be the
greatest thing. And working with people. I've worked with all
kinds of people—the good and the bad, the indifferent. . . . So
that's about the story of it.

*Do you think there's any particular meaning or pur-
pose to life?*

Oh yes. Everybody should have a purpose. If you don't,
you're just wasting your time. I mean that with all my heart. I
felt like I was called to teach, and especially teach the Bible.
And that's been my, and my wife's, biggest joy.

*Is there anything in your life that you wish you'd done
differently?*

No, I don't know as I would. I wish I'd done some things
better. You can look back over your life and see some things
you probably would have liked to change. Otherwise, no.

. . .

When I found out I had cancer, I suppose I felt disap-
pointment. But we all have to expect some sadness and sor-
row. My attitude towards life didn't change after I found out;
at least, not until I couldn't get around. I just went ahead and
did the same things.

. . .

Do you believe there's a heaven or a hell?

There has to be. Did you ever see a battery that didn't have
a negative and a positive? There has to be a heaven and a hell.

Do you have any idea what heaven is like?

It must be a lot better place than this. You can read your Bible and find out a lot about it. But there's a lot of things that Bible writers and Jesus never told us. We know enough about hell that we don't want to go there. I'm looking forward to heaven because things have gotten so bad—even in our own country. We have such a youth problem in all the big cities. And I think they said that the last couple months was the first time there was ever more divorces in America than there was marriages. The sad thing about it is the children they're leaving in broken homes—that's the sad thing about it. And if we don't wake up and get back to what we ought to do, we're going to be in worse trouble.

. . .

I think these problems started in the Second World War—I seen it coming. That's the first time that the mothers ever left the homes. The factories couldn't get enough help. They were hiring even women that were nineteen years old, because their husbands had gone in the service. I seen it coming then—it was breaking up the home. Two things were broken—the wife and the husband were separated, and the children were brought up, sometimes by good people, and sometimes by not good people. And I think that's when our downfall started.

. . .

Do you have any advice for other people about how they should live their lives?

Well, so many times, we're so wrapped up in our own life that we don't have time for others. In 1931, the Salvation Army headquarters had always been in London—that was in the depths of the Depression. They always sent out Christmas letters. They talked about it, and prayed for several days, and de-

125

cided they didn't have the money to send a letter all around the world, so they just sent one word. That word was, "Others."

Whenever we get someplace where we don't think about others, we're in trouble.

. . .

That's the way I feel about life. I still believe we've got to have a great deal of love for others. I think that's the trouble with the world now. Even here in America. Look at how many murders there are. We've lost the love we had for others, and until we get that back, we're in trouble. And it's going to take something more than an ordinary thing to take care of it—we just can't do it ordinary. I'm a Christian, and proud of it. I think if we get back our Christian values, we'll get back to where we belong. I believe that with all my heart. . . .

Look at things in Europe today. In what we used to call Yugoslavia. And Rwanda, down in Africa. I've always liked history, and there never were as many things that were bad as there are today. They claimed they've killed two thousand people in Rwanda in the last week. There's no reason on earth that a man needs to kill his brother because he has a different belief. There just is no reason. We've lost our love for our fellow man.

❦

BRAD DOLEMAN
HOSPICE CARE OF THE VISITING NURSE ASSOCIATION

I'm sixty-nine years old. I was born in Maryland, and grew up in Washington, D.C. I was there until 1941, when I went into the service. . . . I had two brothers and one sister. They're all dead now.

. . .

I never knew my mother. She died when I was nine and a half weeks old, so I never knew her. My dad raised me until I was four years old. He got remarried, and the woman that he married raised me. So in a way, I guess she was my mother. There was a few rough fights along the way, but they weren't too tough on me. There were more good times than there were bad times.

When I was a kid, we didn't have tv, or many of the things we have today, like VCRs. And we didn't worry about it. We just found other things to do. I found it fun to be working. I went to work to have money in my pocket when I was about twelve years old. . . . I did anything that came up—washed windows, carried groceries, sold potatoes.

. . .

I volunteered for the service when I was seventeen. I fought in World War II. It was a little rough, but it was some-thing I was doing for my country. And I felt I shouldn't turn my back on them. I was an Army paratrooper. I jumped at the Bulge, and on D-Day. . . .

D-Day was bloody. I jumped, and some of my friends landed in the water, some of them were wounded, and some of them were dead. You couldn't stop to help them, because if you stopped to help, you'd be holding up somebody else. And you took a chance on getting yourself killed. But I didn't worry about that—I worried about getting that job done. That's what I was there for—to do a job.

. . .

I left the service in 1945. I went back to Washington, D.C. and went to work for a couple hotels. I worked there for five years. Then I went to Chicago and stayed there eight years, working for different hotels in Chicago.

I was a desk clerk. That was interesting—I met all kinds of interesting people.

. . .

I got married when I was forty. My wife died about five years ago. . . . I met my wife on a bus between Washington, D.C. and Alexandria, Virginia. I got to talking to her on the bus. A couple days later I asked her to go out, and she said, "Yes." So we went out. Next thing I know, we got married, moved over to Arlington and had our son.

. . .

We moved here to Kansas City around 1970. My wife was working for [an airline], and she got transferred from Washington, D.C. to Kansas City. Then they told her she had to go to Texas, but I didn't want to go to Texas, so we broke up. I had a job here, and I didn't particularly want to change my job to go to Texas. So she went to Texas—she and my son went to Texas—and I stayed here.

What are the things that have made you the happiest in your life?

Having my son, for one thing. And being able to enjoy my baseball. Because I love baseball. And I guess, meeting some of the people that I deal with. Like the people at the hospital, and the people at the hospice. They treat me like I'm an individual. They've been real good to me. . . .

The lady next door, ever since I've lived here, has always helped me or helped my son when she could, and never asked anything for it. And she not only does it for me, she does it for other people. The woman is a gem.

. . .

I don't really think there's any particular meaning or purpose to life.

Is there anything in your life you wish you'd done differently?

Well, once in a while, I think about one of the first girls I ever went with, and I let her get away from me. Well, I don't regret it in a way, but in a way I do. There's nothing I can do about it now.

I was seventeen at the time. I was still in high school. That was before I went in the service. All the time I was in the service I wrote to her, and she wrote back.

. . .

What type of illness do you have?

Well, I had a slight heart attack. Then they found pneumonia and a tumor—cancer. That's about it, I guess. Emphysema, a little bit of emphysema. They gave me radiation for the cancer and the tumor. They said they're surprised I'm still alive. But I'm still kicking.

December 4 [1993] was the night I was taken to the hospital. I didn't think I was ever going to get out of that emergency room. I was there from 10:30 at night until 5:00 the next morning.

. . .

Has your attitude towards life changed since you got sick?

Well, I try to get along with people. Because I think you only come this way once, and you might as well enjoy the scenery and the people with you.

. . .

Do you have any advice for other people about how they should live their lives?

129

No. Well, I guess just keep your nose out of other people's business and try to help your fellow man. Try to get along with him instead of lying to him. Always be truthful and always be honest. That's all I can say.

. . .

Do you have any particular plans for the future?

Just to live my life the best way I can live it, and see what happens. Hope I live . . . well, I don't want to push the hundred mark. But I already feel that I've had a pretty decent life up to this point.

I look at it this way—when God wants me, He'll come take me, and there's nothing I can do about it. So I guess the best thing to do is to stay here and wait until He comes and gets me. When He wants me, He'll know my address. He won't have to mail me an invitation.

❧

JAMES SCZEPANSKI
HEART OF AMERICA HOSPICE

I'm forty-six years old. I was a freelance photographer. That was my background before I got cancer. I was born in St. Louis, Missouri. I graduated from college here in Kansas City. The place where I live right now is Louisburg, Kansas. That's a small town outside of Kansas City. My wife and I moved here about two years ago, so we could have a couple of horses. I built a house on twenty-five acres of ground out here. My wife's and my major hobby has been riding. We do dressage, combined training—sort of like Olympic-style jumping. And that's what we were doing at the time I was diagnosed with cancer.

. . .

I never rode when I was a child. I only started riding after I met my wife. She was involved with horses, and I took up the hobby to stay along with her.

. . .

We decided to build our own house because we knew we wanted a piece of property that would be well suited to our horses. And when you start shopping for houses in the country, you run across these pretty strange configurations— they're country houses, they look like old farmhouses. And I believed that, with my background in the arts, I could probably design a better house than I could find to buy. And I believe that was the correct decision. . . . It turned out pretty well.

. . .

The way I got involved in photography was . . . actually, my major in college was art—I was a painter. When I got out of college, I decided I couldn't make a living doing fine arts painting, so I got into commercial art and graphic design. From that, a job came open in the company that I worked for as a photographer, and I decided I could do that too.

I did corporate journalism kinds of things—company publications, newsletters, brochures, sales literature. I covered the Olympic torch as it crossed the United States for the 1984 Olympics. I've also done construction project photography on several large projects in the Midwest—things like that.

I enjoyed it very much. It gave me satisfaction watching projects develop and grow. I was planning on pursuing a little bit more of the progress photography as time went on.

. . .

I had one sister—she was killed in a house fire in 1989. I kind of think that contributed a little bit to my cancer—the stress of dealing with that. And shortly after my sister was killed, my mother's health turned bad, so I had to take care of her. And in a way, I became her hospice worker until the time that she died, which was right around the time that I was diagnosed with cancer. So it was kind of an evolutionary process that I should then become a hospice patient. I took care of her while she died.

. . .

I met my wife at a bar. I knew someone who worked in a shopping center where she worked, and one evening I just kind of ran into her. I was with my friend who owned the shop, and she was with a friend of hers. I just struck up a conversation with a corny old bar line, and it went from there. . . .

I said, "Excuse me, but I think I've seen you somewhere before." And she said to me, "Well, I don't recognize you, but I do recognize your friend there." That's how she kind of believed that line. I think she thought it was pretty corny at the time. I mean, she knew what was going on. She's pretty smart.

I was about twenty-nine when we got married. I had been married once before, for seven years. That marriage just didn't work out very well. Then I was single for a couple years.

. . .

We don't have any children. We thought about that quite a bit, and thought about whether or not that would be a good idea. Now of course, it's a little late for that decision. But I think all in all it was a good decision.

. . .

What are the things that have made you the happiest in your life?

There have been a few work projects that have made me pretty happy. And my relationship with my wife has been very rewarding to me. I've enjoyed being married. This sounds corny, but I think I have one of the best marriages—one of the happiest, most secure marriages—that I know of. And that has given me a lot of happiness, peace and quiet. Especially under the current circumstances. She's been really just wonderful at taking care of me, and all through my life.

That has been very rewarding. And I would say that my riding has been very rewarding to me. I've enjoyed that a lot. I'm very happy I got involved in that. . . .

I think the secret to having a good marriage is giving each other enough personal space, and enough personal room to grow. So you don't feel cramped, or that the other person is looking over your shoulder all the time. It takes a long time to get to that position in life. I think we're always tempted to look for the other person's approval. And I would say that it's important not to worry too much about that all the time—to live your own life. And you need to have some luck to kind of click in there, so that the other person gives you just enough approval that you don't feel like they're unhappy with you all the time. You don't want to feel like you're in a competitive situation all the time.

. . .

I don't think there's any particular meaning or purpose to life. I think there's a tremendous amount of chance involved in everyday life. I think that things just tend to happen, and you kind of have to learn to play the cards that you're dealt, and make the best of it. So you're always kind of gambling in life. Life is a gamble, I think. . . .

I can't honestly say there's anything I wish I'd done differently, because I would have missed out on some opportunities that I had because of chance. And those opportunities turned out to be opportunities for transformation. They ended up being chances for me to take a little risk here or there, and try to do something that I had never done before—like, for example, building a house in the country. That was a gamble, and if I hadn't chosen to take that gamble, I would have missed out on something.

. . .

I learned that I had cancer on December 30, 1992. I lost my voice. Along with being a freelance photographer, I was also a part-time teacher in photography at one of the local community colleges. I lost my voice over one weekend, and I thought I had laryngitis, because a lot of people had been catching it at that time. And through a series of tests, we found out that I had [cancer of the lymph node]. . . .

When I found out about it, I was fairly upset, to say the least. I was not prepared for that. I try to look for ways of saying, "Oh yeah, I was really mad about that." But it was just another in a series of things that were happening to me at that time, like the business with my mother and my sister. And I felt like I was having a streak of bad luck, more than anything. . . .

I've managed to accept it pretty well now. I wish that I hadn't had this happen, of course. But I've learned to accept it pretty well. . . .

My attitude towards life has changed since I found out about it. I have learned to live my life one day at a time. That also sounds like a corny thing to say, but that has probably been the biggest development in my life. I was just trying to do too many things on a long range.

How are you feeling now?

You mean, do I accept my circumstances right now? You know, I mean, I'm going to die. And I'm going to die in—oh, I don't know exactly when—but it won't be long. And I have to accept that, because it's pretty much an existential reality. It's just going to happen. And yeah, I accept that. I accept that it's going to happen, and there's not much I can do about it. I wish there were, but there isn't.

. . .

I haven't been able to eat any food at all in probably four weeks or so now. And that's been pretty difficult. . . . I'm not being fed intravenously. That was one of my options. That was one of my last options. My [doctor] wanted me to be fed intravenously, but I decided against that. . . . I felt that, if I had decided to be fed intravenously, I could extend the quantity of my life, but not the quality to a great extent. I just didn't think that it would make for a pleasant life . . . trying to live just on supplements that are going into your body through your veins. And I just decided it was a poor choice. . . .

I've told my doctors they shouldn't take any measures to try to save me. They should not do any kind of CPR. They should not at the last minute come in and try to feed me. There should be no measures taken at all to medically extend my life. When it's time for me to die, I'm going to die. . . .

I don't know if there's a heaven or hell. That question, of course, has come up in my mind, and I believe in a way that the energy that is me—whatever is my essence—will just kind of disassociate at the time that I die. And I don't believe that there will be a heaven or hell, or anything like that. . . .

It's not a frightening thought. At times, it's disquieting. At times, I don't know how to confront that reality. I was raised in the Roman Catholic church, so when I was growing up, I was taught that there was a heaven and a hell. But as I grew up, I didn't really believe that. And so there's kind of a conflict there in my growing up philosophy, and the way I believe now. But no, I don't think there's a heaven or a hell.

. . .

Do you have any advice for other people about how they should live their lives?

135

I believe there is a great tendency toward conflict in the way we live our lives these days. We tend to live our lives on the basis of conflict and resolution. And I personally don't believe in a great deal of conflict. I think that people need to live their lives in a state of peace and acceptance. Of course, you need to resolve conflicts when they arise—you need to do things to confront conflict when it's in your face. But I think that, if you live your life in a state of peace, you will die in a state of peace. I think that, if you live your life one day at a time, seeking peace and harmony with the people you live with, and the situations with which you're confronted, it will make your death much easier to accept when it occurs. . . .

I think that it's something that has to be pursued on a very basic, everyday level. If you try to get along with the world, it will be easier for the world to get along with you.

7

Making Life Interesting

Consideration for others is an important part of life. However, it is also important that we have consideration for ourselves. Life should not be all drudgery and hard work. Instead, we owe it to ourselves to take the time to engage in activities—such as traveling, gardening, or making music—that will bring us joy and help us grow.

TERANCE L. SMITH
ANGELA HOSPICE

I grew up in Garden City, which is a suburb of Detroit. I've lived here all my life. I'm forty-six years old. I'm the oldest of four children. . . . I've got a master's degree in social work. I'm the only one [of the children] who went past high school.

My parents didn't go to college either. My mother only went as far as eighth grade. I think my dad only went to the eleventh grade, but during World War II, anybody that went off to fight in the army, when they came back, they gave them their diploma. So that's how he got his. Everybody else has graduated from high school. . . .

I don't know what made me decide to go to college, other than the kids I hung around with in high school were all going, and I wanted to go too. I was real active in band in junior high and high school. There was some kind of a natural excitement about doing that, and after we got to the point where it was time to go, I realized that I had some skills, but not good enough to really make a go of it with band in college. I did play with them, but I realized that it wasn't going to be my thing to become a band teacher.

. . .

When you went to college, was there something in particular that you thought you wanted to do?

Well, I actually went about it the opposite way. At that point, I knew I didn't want to be a teacher, but I was going to a school where that was their main focus. It was like, I just didn't feel like that was something I wanted to do, but at some point during the four years, I changed my mind and decided I would go. . . . And they had a requirement that, if you were in any kind of an education program, you needed to have some kind of a one-on-one experience. So the assignment they gave me was—there's a children's psychiatric unit at a state hospital not far from the university—so they had me go out there and work with this young man. And I really, really liked it, because I would have to go out and talk with the social worker. And that was kind of what pushed me over [to social work].

I worked twenty-two or twenty-three years, most of it with the state Department of Mental Health, and the last three years with the Board of Education in Detroit as a school social worker.

. . .

When I first got out of school, I worked for the welfare department, in what was then called the Old Age Assistance Program. That was okay, but it was kind of tedious. . . . From there, somebody I knew told me about this job with mental health, so I decided to go ahead and go with that.

I liked it a lot. I think I learned a lot. When you're in college, they give you some general courses on things, but it's really not the same as doing the job. Fortunately, I worked with some people who were very good at what they did, and we got to be friends. So they kind of broke me in on the job and everything.

When I went to the Board of Education, I wasn't too concerned about that, other than that it would be a different kind of place. And it turned out that it was. One of the reasons I went was because I was already starting to have some health problems, and I felt that working at the hospital was going to be too difficult. Of course, I wanted to work as long as I could. The [Board of Education] job was less stressful, and there was more time off because of school holidays and things like that.

I really did not want to leave, but it had gotten to the point where I was having trouble doing the work.

. . .

I liked the job a lot. There was a lot of independence. You had to define what you wanted to do, and then implement it. . . . I would get kids out of class, and we'd sit for half an hour or forty-five minutes, which usually would revolve around playing some kind of game—either a card game or a board game, depending on the age of the kid. You'd do that to facilitate them talking about some other things.

Usually they got referred to me because they were having trouble in school—they weren't cooperating with the teacher, or they were fighting with people, or sometimes I'd get kids because of abuse situations.

. . .

I'm glad I decided to go into social work. I think it ended up being a very good experience for me. . . . I've just had a lot of good experiences, and made good friends.

What are the things that have made you the happiest in your life?

Well, going to school and having a professional career. I think that made me happy. I felt like there was a decent amount of job satisfaction. Beyond that, [my wife] and I broke up ten years ago, and I made a real point of staying in touch with my daughter. I feel like we have a very positive relationship. She's twenty-one. She went away to school for two years, and has kind of dropped out of it. I don't know that her motivation to go is as strong as it needs to be. But she got a taste of college, which is what I wanted. She keeps telling me she's going to go back, and I keep saying, "Okay, let me know.". . . We see each other a couple times a week, and talk on the phone between that.

141

Are there any times in your life that stand out as being especially memorable?

Well, for the last eight years or so, I've financially gotten to a point where my money was not as tight. When [my daughter] was going to college, my money was very tight, because the first year, she stayed in a dorm, and it literally wiped me out. But since then, I've been able to travel and go to some places. Lately, I've been trying to think of somewhere else to go.

I went on a cruise in February. I went from Miami to Cozumel, and Key West. And that was fun. That was a good kind of trip for me to take at that point. When you're on a boat, you don't have to walk anywhere, or not anywhere too far.

I really do enjoy traveling. I went to London a year ago in August. I was thinking about going back there, although I know when I was there before, you had to really walk everywhere. I suppose I could have gone again, but I am having some trouble walking at times. About a week ago, I walked up to the corner to the drug store to get some stuff, and on the way back, I took a dive and fell over.

. . .

I found out I had HIV in 1988. But I had no problems with it until a few months ago. I had been complaining to the doctor about how tired I was all the time, so he agreed I should retire. I retired on the 1st of December, and on the 2nd of December I was in the hospital. . . . They found out I had pneumonia. There had been some symptoms before, but I didn't realize what it was. I had left work one day, and the way I usually come home, they had the freeway closed because of construction or something, so I went on another freeway that would bring me right home, probably in the same amount of time. I ended up in Battle Creek—about 150 miles away. . . . So that was really kind of scary. So I went in the hospital, and

142

it was because, with my lungs being so full, I wasn't getting any air in my brain.

When I was working in the hospital, I worked with people who had all kinds of problems, including dementia, so it was real scary to have that happen.

. . .

I had planned to go rafting on the Colorado River this summer. I did it about three years ago, and had a real good time. But once you get down there, it's five or six days before they can get you out, so I just decided that it's too risky at this point. Maybe when I start feeling a little stronger, I'll be able to do that sort of thing. The same group of people are going to go on a one day trip in West Virginia, but after I fell over, I thought, "Well Terry, you better not be doing that." At least not right now.

But I like to keep active. We do that, and go skiing.

This is a group of friends you have that does things together?

Yes. In fact, that same group of friends is having a retirement party for me at the end of next week. They've all been real good friends, and stay in touch.

Most of them are people I know from working at the hospital. There are a group of people that will come together and be like a family. We're all adventuresome kind of people.

[One of my friends] tried to get me to go skydiving with him. If somebody would throw me out of the plane, I'd probably have a ball, but I can't imagine jumping out of a plane. It was real tempting. He went about twice, and then he decided he'd had enough of that.

. . .

Our group has been taking these trips for eight or ten years at least. We started out by going rafting. The first time, we went with a couple other people, and of course you tell people what you're doing, and they say, "Oh, I want to go when you go again." We ended up renting a bus and driving a busload of people down to West Virginia from here.

. . .

Do you think there's any particular meaning or purpose to life?

Well, I don't know how to answer that kind of question. I think it's real important that people make their lives interesting—that they do things that they're going to find fun. That's why I've always done these trips. You can sit around and be unhappy about different things, or you can make your life interesting. When you go on these kind of trips, they really do wipe you out for a while. But it didn't hurt me. And it's spending some time with people that I like.

Is there anything you wish you'd done differently?

Not particularly. I wish I had started doing this stuff with the stock club when I was about twenty-five. . . . I've been doing that for about the last five years. I've made money, but if I'd started doing this when I was twenty-five . . . . In fact, that's something I've been trying to get [my daughter] to be a part of.

Do you have any advice for other people about how they should live their lives?

To keep themselves active, and make sure they're doing things that they like to do. I think over the years, I've noticed that in other people. They let themselves get all wound up in day to day problems, because they want things this way, or they want things that way. Well, some things, you can't change.

※

LINDA WOOD
ALLEGHENY HOSPICE

I'm forty-nine years old. I live near Pittsburgh, Pennsylvania. I've lived in Pennsylvania all my life. I was born here, got married here and raised my family here. . . . I have four brothers and three sisters. There were a lot of us. . . . I was the oldest of the eight, so I was kind of like a babysitter.

. . .

When I was growing up, I didn't have any goals about what I'd do when I became an adult, because back then, it was kind of closed to women. You either became a nurse or an airline stewardess. There were only certain types of jobs that were considered for a woman.

So did you pretty much think you'd get married and have a family?

I really wasn't thinking too much about it, but I got married when I was eighteen. So I didn't have too much time to consider it. [Laughs.]

I met my husband because he lived down the road from us. So I kind of knew him since I was a little girl. Typical boy next door. His sister was one of my best friends. . . . I have two children—a boy and a girl. They're twenty-five and twenty-four, so they're pretty much on their own.

145

. . .

I worked—I was a bookkeeper. I worked at banks, mostly. I enjoyed it. I really liked working with numbers. Most people think I'm crazy.

What is it in your life that's made you the happiest?

Flowers. I love flower gardens. . . . I do a lot of gardening in my yard. The year before I got cancer, I finished my garden, and I won a prize for it. It went from one extreme to the other—the first year, I got the prize, and the second year, I was sick and couldn't do anything with it, and I was so upset. . . .

I like gardening because it's peaceful. If you go out there and you're in not too good a mood, and you start pulling weeds, it makes you feel better.

Is there anything in particular that's given your life the most meaning?

I think [gardening], and the fact that I live out—not exactly in the country—but we don't have real close neighbors. You don't have anybody watching what you're doing all the time. I enjoy that. . . . We've lived out here for twenty-something years.

Is there anything that you wish you'd done differently?

I think I would have wished that I'd gotten started on my garden sooner. . . . I had a small garden when I was young. My grandmother would give me extra flowers and stuff that she had.

. . .

I found out I had cancer in September of 1992. It was a shock. I thought, it couldn't be cancer. I had a benign tumor before that, so I was hoping it was benign when they found it. But it wasn't.

Early on, I had a lung tumor and a brain tumor, so I had both of those removed. The brain tumor's still gone. The lung tumor keeps horsing around here. So I'll wait and see what it does next.

Do you have any advice for other people?

I think the best way to spend your time is doing something that you really like. Because you don't know how long you have. And if you want to finish something, you should finish it while you have the time.

Do you have any particular plans or goals for the future?

Well, we've been married thirty years, so I think I'd kind of like to go on a trip, like a cruise. That would be something totally different for me. I think I would like that.

Is there anything else you'd like to say?

I'd just like to say that family is very important. They've been great about this whole thing. Because you need somebody.

৯৯

ROY MAYBERRY
VNA HOSPICE

I'm seventy-four years old. I grew up in North Carolina. I come up pretty hard now. . . . I used to have to work, you know, and sometimes my father would wake me up around 3:00 in the morning, and I had to make fires to warm up the house. Sometimes I would be a little slow about getting up when he'd call me to make a fire. I'd put my foot out of my bed, on the floor, and draw it back up. Next thing I know, here come a big belt, with the cover throwed back off of me, and he would really tear me up. He'd tell me, "When I call you, I don't call you but one time."

. . .

Then he used to send us to the spring to get some fresh water. He wouldn't drink no water that had stood overnight. So he'd tell me to go up to the spring and get him some water. And I did that so many times. . . . We had a place down there where we watered the mules, so I thought to myself, "Well, I'm gonna fool him this morning. I'm going down here and dip up a bucket of this water here, and I'm going to bring it up there and give it to him." But he could taste it—he knowed spring water from branch water. So I went down there and I dipped it up, and come back, and he said, "Bring me a drink of that water, boy." So I went and brought the bucket, and he took a drink of it, and he went to smack me in the mouth. He said, "Where'd you get this water at, boy?" I said, "I got it at the spring." And he throwed the bucket so that the handle of it went around my neck, and the water and everything. And he told me, "Boy, you better go get me some water, and you better not be but ten minutes going up there and back."

We'd go on up there to work. He'd put a nickel at the end of the cotton row—we was picking cotton. We'd pick a seven hundred pound bale, without the seeds in it. He'd put a nickel at one end of the row and say, "The first one that gets there can get that nickel." . . . When we'd be going to this cotton patch, we'd leave in the wagon around 3:00 in the morning. When we'd get up to the fields, we'd have to put on our sacks and tie the mules around the wagon.

. . .

Finally, when I got big enough, I got me a job at the rock quarry. I wasn't making but ten cents an hour. My daddy said, "You gotta give me four dollars every two weeks for rent." . . . I went to work around 5:00 in the morning, and it was cold, so I had to put a baby's diaper around my ears, and put my cap down. It was so cold when that moon was shining so bright. So I went to work one morning—it was five minutes past 5:00. The man said, "Go back home, and come back when you can get a full day in." I said, "It's 5:00." I didn't say it was five minutes past 5:00. Well, at ten cents an hour, I lost a whole day there. I was depending on that to help my old man to get some food that we needed.

We had a company store. Everybody who worked at that quarry signed for him to get your check first. When the snow come, you couldn't drill rock, and he'd give you food on time. I didn't know he was this way. He'd get the checks and tell you how much your check was, and then he'd ask you how much you want to pay. I'd bought brand new tires that wasn't but nine dollars then. . . . He said, "Hey Roy, your check is nineteen dollars, how much you want?" And I said, "Oh, I'll pay you about five dollars." And he said, "What did you say?" I said, "I'll pay you about five dollars." And he said, "Since you said that, I'm going to take it all." So he took all my check. I didn't know you had to beg for your money back. I talked to some other people, and I run down to the store and I said, "I never will do that no more. I didn't know I had to ask you whatever you would like to take out and leave me, I'd appreciate it." That's the way you're supposed to say it to him. He had a big cigar in his mouth. He told me, "From now on, whenever I ask you how much you want to pay, then you say—'I'd appreciate whatever you want to take, and leave me the rest'—and there won't be no problem." And I said, "Okay, I'll certainly do that."

. . .

I gotta say this. The white folks down there in them days . . . . You could be standing on the street, and the police would come up and ask you, "Where you work at?" You better not say, "I work for Wright." The policeman would jump out and he'd tell you, "Can't you say Mr. Wright?" "Oh, yes sir, yes sir, I work for Mr. Wright."

It was, "Niggers, they good old niggers." If you got in a fight and got in a little trouble, all you had to do was have a white man. If you worked with those white folks down there, they'd just go down and tell the judge, "Oh, these are good old niggers your honor, he's got a good old daddy." And you'd go free.

. . .

I moved to Greensboro for a time. When I got there, I didn't have nowhere to stay. This service station man gave me a job, for $4.50 a week. He had a two story house—a colored man, him and his wife. He had a car in the back of the service station, with just a shelter over the top. He said, "I'll give you a job, and you can sleep out there in the car. I'll give you some quilts." So I said, "Okay." . . . I didn't think nothing about sleeping out of doors.

I didn't have nowhere to wash my face. . . . I didn't have nowhere to wash my feet. They got to smelling through my shoes. I didn't realize that he could smell 'em, but I didn't think nothing about it. And he said to me, "Hey! Is that your feet smellin' through them shoes?" And I said, "No. . . . I don't know." I'd been keeping my shoes on, sleeping in 'em all night long.

150

. . .

[Mr. Mayberry has been married twice. His first marriage didn't last long. His second marriage has lasted for over fifty years. He worked for many years as a cook and doing domestic work for a number of wealthy people in North Carolina, Connecticut and Cleveland, Ohio. At the time of the interview, he lived in Cleveland.]

. . .

When I was thirty-five or forty years old, I got in a fight with a state trooper. I was fixing to go to [another town], and this truck come upside of me with two people, and they tried to run me off the highway every time I started around 'em. When I got to an intersection of the road, I told him, "Why you trying to make me run off the road?" And I jumped out of the car. And he grabbed one of them pipes out of the back of the truck. About that time, a state trooper come up, and he said, "Hey, hey, what's going on here?" And the man said, "That nigger says I tried to make him wreck!" I said, "You did!" The trooper told me to go get in the car. My brother was with me. And I heard the trooper say, "I'm going to whup him when we get him down there in jail." So I said to my brother, "I might as well take this whuppin' now."

So I got out of the state trooper's car. He said, "I thought I told you to get back in there." My brother got out too. So I said, "You tell me what you gonna take me to town for, 'cause I ain't done nothing. I ain't getting in there until you tell me what you takin' me for." So he said, "I said get back in that car." And I said, "I said I ain't going to get back in there." He had his gun hanging on him too. He hauled off and hit my brother with a blackjack right upside the temple, and he cut a gash about half as long as your finger. I tore his shirt all the way down—every button—broke his gun belt and kicked his gun. Then I ended up going to prison. When I got down to prison, the guards said, "I'd like to have been along there when they done that."

They put me in a rock hole busting rock with a sixteen pound hammer. That was on a chain gang. I was there for about thirty months. I busted rock for nine months in the rock hole.

. . .

I have to tell you about my sickness now. I had my ribs broken in Connecticut in a manhole. . . . In Cleveland, I cracked my ribs again going down the stairs. So it turned into emphysema. I stayed unconscious for two weeks. I didn't know I was in the world. According to the doctors, they'd given me up to die. They had me in intensive care. . . . I don't know how I pulled through. I was unconscious, but I wasn't unconscious, because I could see people looking at me, and I could see tvs and things in each corner, I thought.

. . .

What is it that's made you the happiest?

Oh, let me give you some of this here now. One of the things that has made me happy is, I used to play music. I used to play rock and roll. I'm good with a guitar. . . . I used to walk five miles one way and five miles back—ten miles—to these boys' house. I was born with music in me, and I used to walk to their house to try to teach me how to play a guitar.

I come on up. I got to learn to play the guitar. When I moved to Connecticut, I went to New York on the amateur hour. I could play so well—me and my brother—I passed the amateur hour at the Apollo Theatre. When I went to the amateur hour, the song that I was going to play, some other guy was there, and he started playing it. So I said to my brother, "Lord, I wonder what we gonna do." He got "Go Johnny Go"— that's what I was gonna play. So I thought of a song that I knew—"Things that I used to do, I don't do 'em no more." So I told my brother, "Let's crack down on that one." The people who were sitting back there, they wasn't moving when the other people was up there, but when we started, they got up to walkin' on up there to where we was. And when I quit playing that one, they told us to go on through. We come out of there at 3:00 in the morning.

The manager would say, "Always go out and come back sober and sound." But I told him, "I ain't gonna be drunk, but I got to tear this guitar up. I got to really let it go." . . .

They had a clown down there that would shoot you off, but he never shot me off. . . . Music is my hobby, and I can rock guitar.

Do you still play?

Well, I'm sitting here looking at my guitar right now. But I ain't been out since I got sick. I can still play like I used.

When I was in Connecticut, a record company give me a contract. . . . I come to find out they were going to give me four percent per side per record per year. But under the contract, they could sell me to any company and still pay me four percent per side, and probably sell me out for eight percent per side, so I wouldn't sign no contract. So I just let it go and played around in clubs. It wasn't for money—sometimes I just played for fun.

Do you think there's any particular meaning or purpose to life?

Oh yeah. The people who are out in this world in this life now, to me, I would say they're lacking a lot in knowing life, and knowing what life is about. People don't think about tomorrow. . . . In my day and time, you went to church, and you heard what the preacher preached about, and you'd have to turn around and tell your parents when you got home what he preached. People now doesn't look at life, and some of 'em don't know what it is to be back in them days when I come up. Your life is everything to you while you're here, but people today don't seem to appreciate even what life is. My life, since I got sick, is knowing there's a God somewhere. But today, people thinks that there ain't no God. If you just put your trust in Him, He will see you through.

. . .

Today, there's this killing and robbing. . . . This world is messed up now. I've often thought that I need to get in the church so I can help out and tell what the Lord is doing for people today.

. . .

My life is happy, even until now, because I got something to be thankful for—being able to pull through, and still living. And I often think to myself, there's something God got for me to do.

☀

8

Vices

Taking the time to enjoy life and continue to grow is one aspect of being considerate of oneself. Another, which is equally important, is avoiding conduct that is self-destructive. The urge for instant gratification can at times seem irresistible. We would do well to remember, however, that, as demonstrated in the following interviews, activities that may seem pleasurable at the time can ultimately be the cause of great pain and regret.

JOSE FERRER
FAMILY HOME HOSPICE

I'm forty-six years old. I grew up in Spanish Harlem in New York City, on 112th between Park and Madison. I lived in New York until I was around thirty-five or thirty-six. Then I moved out to San Diego. And from San Diego, I moved here to Las Vegas.

I moved to San Diego because my ex-sister-in-law told my ex-wife that if you put New York know-how in San Diego, you could get over like a fat rat. New Yorkers are supposed to be fast talkers and everything else. I didn't want to leave, but the old lady wanted to leave at that time, so we just packed up and moved out to San Diego.

I was in San Diego up until 1988—around five years. Then my second wife wanted to move out to Las Vegas, so we moved out here.

. . .

I was an only child. My mother died from an abortion after me, back in the old days of coat hanger abortions. She bled to death. Then my father remarried. . . . I have a brother and a sister in Puerto Rico, and one brother in New York.

I was one and a half when my mother died, so I really don't remember anything about her. . . .

Growing up in New York, I used to play in Little League. Even though they claimed we were poor, I never missed a meal. My grandparents were the ones that raised me—my grandparents and my aunt. They took care of me very well.

I went through elementary school. I had gotten a spelling

bee award. I went to junior high school as an honors student.
I had a pretty good child life.

. . .

When I was in New York, I did janitorial work and window
cleaning. My apprenticeship was the Empire State Building.
They started me on the fifth floor and worked me going up, so
I could get used to the height. . . . I worked on the World Trade
Center. I did the construction cleaning on that, which was the
first cleaning. . . . I worked at Fordham University in the Bronx.
I started as a regular custodian, and I made assistant supervisor, supervisor, assistant branch director. And while I was
there, I went to school and got a couple of AAs, and became
director of the maintenance department.

After that, I went to San Diego, following the ex-old lady.
When I was in San Diego, I stayed with the janitorial work.
And then I got into civil service in the Naval station in San
Diego. I started as a clerk, and at the same time I was working
janitorial at night. Then I started working as a laborer. . . . I
went from a laborer to a pipefitter helper. When I was a pipefitter helper, I started drinking a whole lot. I became . . . well,
I'm an alcoholic. It started to affect my job—I wasn't going to
work. So after a while, I landed up in San Jose, California. I
worked there at the school district as a janitor for six or eight
months. And then I met my wife here in Vegas, because we
had separated because of my drinking.

When I came to Vegas, I was working at the University of
Las Vegas—UNLV—as a janitor. And then I started drinking
again and I lost that job. And then I got a job at the University
medical center. I'd been there for four years, until January or
February, when I got sick and I couldn't work anymore.

. . .

I married my first wife when I was in my early thirties. She
used to work in a drug program. I was a patient in the pro-

gram, so we started seeing each other from there. Our marriage didn't last long—probably two years.

I met my second wife in a singles bar. We've been married ten or eleven years.

We don't have any children.

. . .

What are the things that have made you the happiest in your life?

Well, I don't think there is anything really. [Laughs.] I really don't think there is anything. Especially now, when I've ended up with this disease.

Do you think there's any particular meaning or purpose to life?

There has to be. If one applies himself to be something, or to do something for himself.

Is there anything you wish you'd done differently?

Oh, of course. No drugs and no alcohol. . . . I got involved in that when I was in the military. I joined the military when I was nineteen. I was a medic in the Navy. I landed in Vietnam, and I was shooting my own self up with morphine. I came out of the military just before they started getting the blood and urine tests. They started giving the tests in 1970, and I was out in 1969, and I just continued the same pattern of drinking and drugs.

. . .

Vietnam was one heck of an experience. One learns a lot about oneself, survival-wise, and you learn a lot about people.

159

When we were under fire, a lot of people used to break up, and then other people used to just take charge.

I was in combat situations—I was a Navy medic going out on patrols with the Marines.

I was in the military for close to two years. When Tricky Dick came in, he got me out of 'Nam with early cuts. . . . They wanted to re-enlist me because, according to them, I was military material. I had gotten up to the rank of E-5, which was Sergeant. I made it two times. I got busted. Since I was a medic, I couldn't carry a rifle. I was just supposed to carry a sidearm, which was a .45. And they busted me down. My excuse for that was, I'm not gonna be shot at, and I can't shoot back—my bullet is going to fall right in front of them, and they're gonna laugh at me and shoot me between the eyes.

I don't know. As far as regretting the service . . . I learned a whole lot when I was in the service. . . .

Going into battle was scary like hell. Scary like hell. You had to change your underwear. . . . I used to go out on patrol for weeks. We used to stay out for one or two weeks, come back in for four days, and then go back out. It was like a constant thing. . . . At the time, it was hard to deal with. After a while, it becomes like going to work. You get up in the morning, you get dressed and just go to work. When you're finished, you come back to the camp, and you're off.

Were you always worried that you might get killed?

Yeah, the thought used to cross my mind. [Laughs.] The thought always crossed my mind—whether it would be the last patrol or whatever.

So how would you deal with that?

Drugs.

. . .

160

When I came back to the States, it was pretty hard adjusting. I remember one time, I was with my grandmother—she was sixty-five or sixty-six. We were coming out of the subway. A truck backfired, and I pushed her right down on the doggone steps.

I didn't go for any type of counseling or anything. I just came right out and tried to get used to civilian life. It was hard in the beginning, but after a while I just forgot about everything.

. . .

I have AIDS. I found out I had it three years ago. . . . It was a surprise when I found out. You worry about your spouse—whether you've infected her. But she's okay.

How did you feel when you found out?

Get ready to die.

Has your attitude towards life changed at all since you found out you had HIV?

Yes. Just trying to enjoy whatever, and just trying to take it easy now. . . . Right now, I'm in pain. I just got out of the hospital a month and a half ago. I was in for a month.

Do you have any advice for other people about how they should live their lives?

Yeah. As far as drugs and alcoholism—do not partake. And try to live life to the utmost.

. . .

I don't really have any plans for the future. Just trying to get day by day. Because now tomorrow is not promised to me at all. Well, it isn't promised to anyone. But with this disease, it's not promised at all.

161

Are you religious at all?

Half and half, I would say. I strayed away from religion.
But I know there's a supreme being. . . . I haven't become any
more religious lately. I wasn't that religious before. I don't believe that, just because I'm sick with this disease, I should run
right away and become a born-again Christian. If I wasn't before, why should I do it now, just because I'm going to die? To
me, that's being hypocritical.

SARA
FAMILY HOME HOSPICE

I was born in Omaha, Nebraska on January 6, 1913. I'm eighty-
one years old. I was born of Jewish parents. My father was
Lithuanian, my mother was Russian. I had two brothers and one
sister. The older brother passed away five years ago. I have one
brother living in Omaha, and a sister in California. . . .

I've smoked since I was seventeen. I stopped about three
years ago. I had heart trouble, and I stopped smoking. I was
in a restaurant one day with a friend, and I started to cough
and I almost choked. I had a biopsy and found out I had cancer of the throat. That was in January of 1993. I don't know
how long I have to live. I haven't had another biopsy since. I'm
living in a retirement hospital, and they do as much as they can
to keep me going.

I lived in Omaha most of my life. I was married in 1934.
My husband died when he was fifty-three. . . . He had dia-
betes. . . . He died very suddenly. . . .

I met my husband at a dance. I was working in a grocery

store as a bookkeeper and an order clerk, and I quit my job and went to Chicago to stay with cousins. And they took me to a dance, and I met him there. I came back to Omaha. He went to CCC camp. He went back to Chicago when he got out. He had a falling out with his parents, so he came back to Omaha with me. We got married on January 28, 1934. I have two boys. One is fifty-nine and one is forty-nine. The oldest boy has been married and has two children—two girls—and three grandchildren. The youngest boy has been married for twenty-five years. He has two children—one girl and one boy. My youngest boy lives in Colorado, and the oldest one lives in Las Vegas.

. . .

When my husband died, I was working for an importing company, for fifteen years. When he died, I stayed in Omaha for two years. The weather was so bad one winter, I decided I didn't want to live in cold weather anymore. My oldest son was going to college in Tucson, so I went to see him. I came to Las Vegas on my way and decided I liked Las Vegas, so I came here to live. . . . I've been here since 1969 and I like it very much. I've made loads of friends.

I worked for the Flamingo Hilton as a credit clerk. I worked for the Las Vegas Hilton for nine years as a credit clerk. And then I retired, and I went to work for city hall for ten years. I retired from there three years ago.

. . .

I'm a very active person. I don't like being tied up in a room. . . . I'm getting feedings every night, and sometimes it lasts until about 8:30 in the morning. I have no way to eat anymore, and I have a G2 tube which I get fed through. I don't have any way to chew, so they've made an incision in my stomach, and I have a tube, and it's connected to a feeding tube that I eat through. I eat regular meals, but they're all liquid. For breakfast, I get cereal and tea. For lunch, I get soup, tea and a dessert—all soft. And for dinner, I get the same thing.

It's a very boring way to eat, but there's no other way I can eat. There's no way to swallow, because I would choke.

What are the things that have made you the happiest in your life?

My marriage was a very, very pleasant thing. I enjoyed being married. My husband was a delightful person to be with. He had two ways to look at life—right and wrong. And if you didn't do it right, then you were wrong. . . . My children give me a lot of pleasure. And my work. And I love people. No matter what. I don't care who they are or what they do—as long as they don't ask me to do it, they're my friend. I love people.

When I quit city hall, I got a get well card when I went to the hospital, and there were forty-five names written on it telling me to get well. I make friends very easily. I've made friends here in the hospital. They say I do a lot of good things. I try to help people, but I like everybody. I don't hate anybody. There's no hate in my life.

Do you think there's any special meaning or purpose to life?

Well, right now, I'm just trying to get along every day. Some days I would like it to be finished, because I'm not too well some days, and I don't feel too good. And my throat is starting to bother me more than it had in the beginning. And it's hard for me to swallow. But I try not to show it. Every once in a while I get very depressed, and I cry. And the hospice helps me. . . .

Is there anything in your life you wish you'd done differently?

I'd like to change that I don't have cancer. That I would like to change. I would like to be my old self again, because I still have a lot of energy, and a lot of things to do. I still want to live a good life, and not so tied up here. I'll be here the rest of my life. I would like to change that, but there's no way. But otherwise, my marriage was beautiful, my children are very good. They've never been on drugs, they've never been gambling, they've never done things that they've been arrested for or gotten in trouble. They both went to college. They're very lovely boys.

. . .

Do you have any advice for other people about how they should live their lives?

Yes—don't smoke. No matter what. You think it isn't hurting you—you don't really know. Don't smoke.

I can't tell them what else to do. I didn't lead a perfect life. I wouldn't say that I was the best person in the world. But I know I didn't do anything else that was bad.

. . .

Do you think there's any secret to having a good marriage?

Yeah, all you have to do is say, "You're right," and they've won the argument. But you can still be right. My husband and I had our ups and downs. . . . We were very, very close. I enjoyed his company. Our sex life was good, and the money was available. We had a nice house. My husband liked good things, and we bought the best. He came from a family that wasn't very wealthy, and mine wasn't either. So when we bought, we bought the best. Our marriage was very good. Very good.

માર્ક

9

Appreciating the Gift of Life

Perhaps the most important lesson to learn from these interviews is that we should not take our lives for granted. Although some of us are more fortunate than others, we all have something for which we should be thankful, whether it be the love and support of our family and friends, a job that is fulfilling and challenging, or simply the ability to appreciate a warm, sunny day or moonlit night. Even though we all must face certain hardships and disappointments, we should not let them blind us to all the positive things in our lives. We need to recognize what is truly important and avoid wasting our time worrying about things that are ultimately insignificant. In the end, we are only here for a very short time—we should try to make the most of it.

HARRY ANDERSON
McKENZIE-WILLAMETTE HOSPICE

I originated in western Iowa seventy-nine years ago. I live in Springfield, Oregon. I came to Oregon in 1940, with a wife and three children. I have one brother and one sister—they're older than I.

The main reason for coming west was, my parents and everybody else had a college education. I didn't, and I wanted my children to have a college education. I didn't see how I could do that in a small Midwestern town, so we thought we would come to Eugene, where they had a university.

When you were a kid growing up, did you have any idea what you wanted to do when you became an adult?

You mean as a life work? Not really. I've always been behind the eight ball. I worked because I had to, not because I wanted to.

When I came to Oregon, I started working in a sawmill. Then I worked in the shipyards during World War II. After that, I spent most of my life in powerhouses, generating electricity—thirty-one years. . . . I didn't really like my jobs—I'm lazy. Work was never my first priority.

. . .

I got married when I was in Iowa. My wife and I were from the same small town—1,500 people.

Have you known your wife pretty much all your life?

169

Well, you don't notice little girls when they're ten or twelve—you wait until they grow up a little bit. She was still in high school when I first knew her, and we got married soon afterwards. We had three children in a comparatively short time.

. . .

We moved to Oregon because I had a friend who had come out here. Trying to keep a family going on ten dollars a week, even in those days, was not really that great a living. And this fellow said, you come out to Oregon, and one of the big pluses was that fifty-four percent of the state would belong to me—national forest land or Bureau of Land Management land. So I had access to fifty-four percent of it, without anybody telling me, "No." And when you come from a state where everything is privately owned, public land is a big plus.

So that was one thing. He said living was very reasonable—you could get fresh vegetables, and there were lots of fish, lots of deer, and wood was cheap. So it was a cheap place to live, and there was access to the university.

We did lots of outdoor activities. We used to backpack. We still fish. I quit hunting about fourteen years ago.

. . .

What are the things that have made you the happiest in your life?

The outdoors. Conservation. I'm very interested in conservation, environmental problems. Birds, fish and trees. Those are the things I'm most concerned about.

I enjoy my health now, with this cancer I had.

Are you recovered from that?

It depends on who you talk to. I think I'm doing fine. My family doctor doesn't give me positive encouragement about a full recovery. He thinks I still have the potential for pancreatic cancer. . . .

I first found out I had cancer in March. I don't have it—that was the gist of my problems. Pancreatic cancer starts out with severe itching—spots all over your body. It hurts like hell. That probably started in January or February. By March, it was getting intolerable, so I went to a doctor, and he sent me to a [specialist]. They said I had an obstructed bile duct.

. . .

[Mr. Anderson described an operation where he had a number of medical devices placed in his bile duct.]

Between March 15 and April 15, they [implanted four devices] and a sheath. And I was very ill. They said, "You're so bad, we want to put in another one tomorrow." And I said, "To hell with it. You've put in four of them. They haven't done any good, and I want to go home. If I'm going to die, I want to go home and look at the birds, and squirrels and flowers." They said, "If you go home, you'll be dead between ten and thirty days."

So I went home, and the way I tell the story is, the next week, me and the grim reaper glared at each other, and he blinked, and I got better. . . . I've been slowly getting better. I was very weak until the last week or ten days.

. . .

I'm not afraid to die. I'm seventy-nine years old—I've seen a lot happen. My kids have grown up. They all have good jobs, they don't need me. It's a little hard on my wife—she's younger than I, and she's in very good physical condition. I said, "You go on with your life. Don't be worrying about me." The bottom line is quality of life. I said, "I will not take chemo." I took care of a gal who had a malignancy that couldn't be operated on, and she lived for fourteen months in a lot of pain. . . . It finally got to the point where they were feeding her through her nose. She literally starved to death—she couldn't assimilate any food.

171

So the hell with that. I've seen too many people . . . . I think in the next twenty years, they'll find that chemotherapy is in the same category as surgeons did 150 years ago when they bled people to cure something they didn't know anything about.

. . .

Has having gone through this near-death experience changed the way you look at life?

Because of the type of work that I did, I never was a social person. I never had a large group of friends. The few friends that I had were very special. But since we retired, we've joined retired groups of people that travel, and look at birds, and trees and water—things like that. I've met a lot of people.

When I got this problem, I got the most wonderful response—cards, letters, telephone calls. I'm still getting them, and I'm well as far as I'm concerned. And the support that I got from my contemporaries was undoubtedly a big plus in my recovery.

The things that I appreciate now, I don't know that I appreciate any more [than I used to], because I was not scared to die. The hell with it—if I'm going to die, I'm going to die. This is not a fatalistic attitude. . . . A lot of different religions believe it's all foreordained. And of course we have sayings here: "If you're born to be hung, you're not going to die from having your throat cut." So that's the way it goes. The thing you have to do is not worry.

. . .

Do you have any advice for other people about how they should live their lives?

Yes. Be satisfied with what you have, and what you are. And don't feel bad that you are not the thing that maybe your parents wanted you to be, or even that you started out to be. Because enjoyment of life is very important.

When the hippies came to Oregon in the 1960's—sure, a lot of them were strictly drug people—but we had some great ones. We had a guy come out here, and he makes batik. He's good enough that he has batik in the Smithsonian. We have some excellent bronze casting people. There's a couple that lives down in the woods here, where a lot of them ended up, and they make $3,000 sleeping bags. They don't just measure your physical dimensions—they check your metabolism and that kind of stuff. They're five to ten years behind in their orders—for people that climb Everest and places like that—but they don't worry about it. They just make enough to live the way they want to live, and the hell with it.

. . .

[Mr. Anderson mentioned the slogan, "A mind is a terrible thing to waste."]

If you've got the smarts, it's too damn bad that you can't take advantage of it. Which is my problem. I probably have the brains, but I'm lazy. But I can recognize that and say, "Okay, I'd just as soon enjoy Oregon, and sit on my rear end and bitch about the way the state's being run." That's the way it goes.

IRENE BATTLE
McKENZIE-WILLAMETTE HOSPICE

I'm sixty years old. I live in Springfield, Oregon. I grew up in southeastern Idaho. I was the baby of a family of six. The oldest was eighteen years older than I. The next one to me was seven years older. I have one sister seven years older, and another sister fourteen years older, and then the three brothers, sixteen, seventeen and eighteen years older.

I grew up on a farm. My parents are immigrants from Russia. They're of German ancestry. My mother was eighteen when she came to the U.S. My dad had come earlier. I think he was still in school. They met in the Dakotas, where so many immigrants ended up. They came over and homesteaded in Idaho. And from there, we all scattered.

. . .

When I was born, my brothers were ready to go off to university. Everybody scattered, so I grew up more or less an only child. I'd see them when they'd come home on vacation.

. . .

I didn't like living in Idaho—I hated the hot and dry. I love Oregon. I love woods and greenery. So basically, right down to my core, I didn't like it over there.

When I was eighteen, I went from Idaho to Los Angeles. I spent about thirty years there. I went to Los Angeles for nurse's training. I had been in Pocatello, and I didn't think too much of it. It didn't seem right to me. I wanted to go to a bigger school, so I went to Los Angeles.

Before I got into school, I had to work. And like a young brat, you get to working, and have your own money, and then you kind of lose your ideals.

I worked for Pacific Telephone. But I did go to night school, and got a license as a cosmetologist. Although I never worked at it.

. . .

I loved Los Angeles. It was beautiful in those days. . . . I lived in Santa Monica for a while, and then closer downtown.

. . .

I got married when I was thirty-three. I met my husband because he lived nearby. I have one son. He's in the Air Force. He's stationed in Illinois. They're having a child in a few months.

. . .

We decided to come to Oregon because my husband was retiring at that time, and we'd heard really good things about Oregon—quiet and woodsy, and no big crowds. And that's how it was here. . . . It was good for our son. The schools were much better here. Now it's getting wilder. He was here at a good time. That's probably the main reason we moved up here.

Do you have any hobbies?

Just reading. I do a lot of needlecraft. That's about all. I used to garden when I could—I can't do that anymore. . . .

I think the thing that's made me the happiest is my son, and seeing his accomplishments. It was a worthwhile project.

Do you think there's any particular meaning or purpose to life?

That's very difficult. . . . Not really, unless we make it ourselves. There isn't just naturally a purpose, no. . . .

I believe in a greater being, but not in organized religion. My interest is in Religious Science. I was introduced to it through friends in Los Angeles. Although I don't go to church now, it is still the one thing that makes sense to me. It's compatible with just about any other religion. . . . Within everyone is the power for self-healing. . . . Anything is possible, as long as you don't interfere with the laws of nature. There has been self-healing, but you're never going to say there isn't going to be death, because there has to be—that's natural.

. . .

I don't really believe there's a heaven or hell. I don't think we're going to one place or the other. I don't know what happens to people when they pass away, but I think that life continues on another level, somehow. To go any further, I think it would take somebody who has studied it. I haven't.

Is there anything in your life that you wish you'd done differently?

I've thought a lot about that. If we'd changed anything, we would have missed out on some of the good stuff. So it's best to just leave it alone.

. . .

I have terminal breast cancer. It's metastasized. I had my first bout with it in a mastectomy eleven years ago. They first diagnosed that it had metastasized in March of last year. When I first found out about it, I was quite devastated. Quite frightened.

How have you been dealing with that?

I just don't dwell on it. I just have to take every day at a time. I just don't think about it. I didn't know before when I was going, and I still don't know. I just carry on as before. . . .

I think my attitude towards life has changed. The same things aren't important to me. I can see I attached great importance to silly little things before. Most things aren't that important. . . . The things that are important are caring between people. The quietness of sharing. Most of us aren't going to do great or renowned things on this earth. But we can sure be nice to the next guy. That's important. Trying to prove you're better than somebody else just for the sake of it is rather worthless. Showing off your personal possessions—that's worthless.

176

Do you have any advice for other people about how they should live their lives?

Don't work so hard at it. It's okay to relax a bit.

. . .

Last June, [the doctors told me] I had less than three months. But I'm still plugging along. . . . How that came about, I don't know. . . . Perhaps it just wasn't time yet.

Do you have any plans for the future?

No, I don't do that. I more or less think of being ready. Cleaning up and being ready.

ॐ

LEMUEL BRAITHWAITE
CABRINI HOSPICE

I was born in Manhattan, West 140th Street, seventy years ago—1923. I've lived in New York all my life.

I like living in New York. I wouldn't change it for nothing in the world. I love New York. I don't care to go any other place. . . . New York, you have to learn to love it. You learn to love it if you came up in it. I learned to love it. It didn't ever treat me bad. I accepted what it had to give, and I gave what I had to give. I enjoyed it. . . . It was just good to me. So I was good to it.

I never cared to go anywhere else. . . . New York is home to me. . . . New York is a place where, if you come up in it, you have to love it.

. . .

[Mr. Braithwaite described the effects of cancer.]

I lost a lot of weight. I lost eighty pounds. This is the smallest I've been since I was twelve. I weigh 140 pounds. I usually weigh 230—I kept that the better part of my life. . . . I never remember being this small. But I guess that's life. You can't stop it.

. . .

You can't let it get you down. You can't go into a depression. But it'll make you feel like that. . . . This is one of the times I was sick in my life. For the better part of my life, I was never sick. . . . When I got to sixty-eight, I had a minor heart failure. Then when I was coming out, this mass on my neck was swollen up. So they took a biopsy, and found out it was cancer.

. . .

It ain't the worst thing in the world. Some people hear "cancer," they panic. Which they got something to panic about. But I guess it's just like anything else. They got a whole lot of things worse. If you think you got it bad, you look at somebody else. . . .

They have tough times in this world; good times in this world. So you just have to accept it and go along. When you get a little age on you, you can take it by day. Because you never think things will happen to you. Things happen. If you survive long enough, something's gonna happen. You can put a bet on that. But that's only because it's life. Life, you can't know too much about. 'Cause if you know too much about life, then you'll get miserable. And you don't want to be miserable. So you know just enough. You know as much as you want. Otherwise, you seek and you shall find. . . .

But you keep on grappling, because you want to survive.

You want to survive without pain. But pain go along with it. When you get the age, pain go along with it. But they say you can be halfway comfortable with the pain if you have it, because modern science has made it that way.

. . .

Do you think there's any particular meaning or purpose to life?

I don't know. . . . I imagine we're here for something. . . . You have to be fortunate to know what your purpose in life is. . . . We were put here for something. Some good reason. Good or bad—there was a reason. We just wasn't put here. You just might never know what you were put here for. . . . What you do, you enjoy the little bit that you have. That's what it's all about.

What are the things that have made you the happiest in your life?

I had a few enjoyable things in life. I never had all the money I needed. I know what money is. But I had enough. I enjoyed it. Enjoyed spending it. Enjoyed it when I was getting it.

I had a couple of marriages that were good. I enjoyed it. Enjoyed the kids. I appreciated life a little bit. I loved it.

My last wife, I was married thirteen years. My first one, I was married about thirty years. It was all right.

My first one, I was raised with. We came up together. There was no problems. . . . The second one, she was enjoyable. I had a good relation with her. Can't be fortunate all the time. She died New Year's Day [1976]. . . . We went to a dance. . . . She was taking hypertension pills. When she came home, she took the pills . . . and went to sleep. And that was it. . . . When you're drinking, and then you're taking those pills, when you

179

go to sleep, you ain't got nothing to fight with. If she had stayed up, she would have been okay.

That's life. You can't hold life. You can't stop it. Things happen to you that never happened before.

. . .

I have three kids. I got a few more. My name won't rest. I got more than a few grandchildren. I told you that the name will go on. If I was looking for my name to go on, it'll be here.

What kind of work did you do?

When I was working, the most work I did was construction. Because it was easy. Easy when you're young. It don't bother you. Work hard, stay up all night, when you're young. And when I found out that I couldn't work hard and stay up nights, I quit. . . . I liked it, because it came easy. I was a mason—I laid bricks. It wasn't nothing that hurt me. Because I knew whatever hurt me, I was going to quit. I wasn't going to work, and let it tear me down. So when it got too much, I didn't retire—I quit. I was good with my hands, so I could do most anything.

After the construction, I did several things. I worked on pictures. I worked security, and I worked acting a few times. I was making more for security than for acting. The last movie I worked on was "The Cotton Club." I did security. . . . The Cotton Club was on 142d Street, originally. When I was a kid, I seen it because I was raised right there—two blocks away. It was a big time club. But it was for whites only. It was a white club in Harlem. And no blacks allowed. I never went in there.

. . .

Is there anything you wish you'd done differently?

Not really. I was never one to turn the clock back. There's no turning back. I enjoyed the little bit I had. No regrets. I wouldn't have done it any different, because I didn't know no different. I did the little bit of things that I wanted to do, and I enjoyed it.

Are there any moments in your life that stand out?

Outstanding? There wasn't nothing too outstanding. All the outstanding things I did were normal. I just enjoyed it. I enjoyed the little bit of time I had. Might have a year or two more. If I do, that's okay. If I don't, I'm missing something. It don't worry me. I got to be a ripe old age. Who would have figured I'd get to be seventy? They say that's a ripe age. A lot of people don't make it.

Who can say how long he'll survive? But if you survive, you enjoy it. I told you I didn't have too many suffering days. I can't say the end is near, because I'm still surviving. And right now, I don't mind surviving, because it's the only life I know. Don't care to know any other one—if there's another one. I'll fight to carry on this one.

My life has changed. But that ain't nothing. It had to change.

Life, enjoy it all you can. Because when you look at it, it's short. Time passes by fast. . . . You never know. You never, never know.

৵

DR. STEPHEN A. GRACE
ANGELA HOSPICE

I grew up in the small town of Redford, which is about twelve miles from the city of Detroit. Along with the rest of my family, their mothers and fathers before them were more or less pioneers in that area. I had one brother and one sister; they're both deceased. I'm the youngest of three. I'm eighty-two years old.

. . .

I like the Detroit area. I was born and raised there. It's changed a lot since I was a boy, but it's still home.

. . .

Do you have any particular memories of your childhood days?

Well, I always thought that they were very ordinary. We used to go up north. My dad had bad hay fever, so he'd work the rest of the year, and then on August 15, we'd take off for Lake Huron, and stay there until the hay fever season abated.

. . .

We did the usual things for fun when I was a kid. We roller skated a lot, and played ball. At night when we didn't have anything else to do, we'd go downstairs and pop some corn, or crack some hickory nuts, or eat some apples and call that a night. Not too much excitement in those days. We stayed home more in those days.

We finally picked up a radio when they came in so as you could hear it. I remember my dad bought an Atwater-Kent that stood so high, and we'd turn the volume up and really enjoy it. It was quite amazing to me. It still is. I still don't understand the television. . . .

When I was a kid, I didn't really have any idea what I'd do when I grew up. I started floundering around, like so many of us. I was out of high school, and working in a gas station that my brother owned. He and his partner owned a gas station that was very successful for almost fifty years. So it was easy to get a job there, and it wasn't far from home, so I kind of loafed there. . . . Then I met a chiropractor friend of mine who talked me into going up to school. I'm not a very tall person, and I said, "They don't want little shrimps like me—they want big guys." He said, "Well, it isn't in the size, it's in the technique." So he pestered me several times, and finally I surprised him one day and said, "Okay, I think I'll go to Davenport and take up chiropracting." Which I did.

I was just seventeen—very young. It was a four year course. So when I came out, I was pretty green. In fact, I had to wait from March 6 to March 29—that's my birthday—to get my diploma, because I wasn't twenty-one.

I got a very early start, but a very slow start. I found it very difficult. Like they say at the races, I didn't get out of the gate very fast. It took us a long time.

I married, and had four children, eleven grandchildren and thirteen great-grandchildren. Someone asked me if I believed in Santa Claus, and I said, "I am Santa Claus."

. . .

I came back and opened a practice in Birmingham, Michigan. I went there thinking that's where all the money was—Birmingham's considered quite a fancy town. Well, it was a fancy town, but it was too fancy for me. I died there. I just couldn't hack it at all. So I gave up there after a couple, three months, and then I moved to an area called [Brightmore]. I managed to get a start there, but it was a very slow start. In fact, for a while, I worked at Ford for eighteen months so I could eat.

I didn't know my folks didn't have any money. See, the banks closed when I graduated, so everybody was broke, in-

cluding myself, so I just had to go to work. So I worked at Ford
for eighteen months, and tried to practice in the evening. Well,
I put together a few dollars and a few war bonds, and I bought
a fella out, and finally got a very slow start. My wife used to
say, "We're poor, but nobody knows it."

It was difficult, but of course, I couldn't have done it without my wife—she was seventy-five percent, me twenty-five
percent. She never complained. She never got in my way, or
tried to tell me what to do, or said, "Go out and get a real job"
or anything. She stuck with me. If it wasn't for her, I don't think
I would have made it.

. . .

I met my wife on the telephone, by accident. Somebody
heard me say I was looking for a girl to take to a bowling ban-
quet. It just happened that this girl was visiting her father, and
she called me up and said, "I'm down at my dad's place, and
I want you to meet this girl." So she put me on the wire. I
made a date immediately—I fell in love with her voice.

I knew right away that she was the one. There was no
question about it. I was twenty-eight years old, she was
twenty-six. So we were just the right age to get married. . . . I
met her in the latter part of March or first of April, we were engaged in April, and married the following January.

So that was how I met her, and we've been married now
for fifty-three years. She has Alzheimer's now.

. . .

I worked through the Depression, trying to make ends
meet. That's why it was so difficult. The chiropractic profession
was not as well known then as it is now, and a lot of people
were skeptical of it. And of course, our prices were ridicu-
lous—two dollars a call. It didn't add up very fast.

We were just one step ahead of the welfare there for a little while, but we managed. We never did fall off the wagon.
And gradually it increased. My wife was a private secretary for

the steel company, and the rules were then that when you got married, you got fired. So she couldn't work. But then later on, when our family was grown, she picked up a job and worked at the Detroit Institute of Arts, which was a very lovely job. Of course that helped the financial situation quite a bit.

. . .

I enjoyed being a chiropractor. The best thing I can think of would be if I could go to my office today. I knew my patients very well, and I treated them as a friend, as well as a patient. That isn't the ideal way. In fact, I always considered myself a poor businessman. I was a better chiropractor, but a poor businessman. Today, it seems like the doctors are better businessmen than they are doctors.

. . .

What are the things that have made you the happiest in your life?

Well, when I got people feeling good. When I had patients who were in extreme pain, and they'd walk out painless—those were the highlights of my life. Because that was the only thing I ever really did—it seems like I've been a chiropractor since I was born. And to see people become well, and meet them on the street, and they'd say, "Boy, I sure feel great after you took care of me." Those were the highlights.

Do you think there's any particular meaning or purpose to life?

I never quite figured it out. We're put here, and we just have to scratch our way through it. And sometimes it's pretty cruel.

Is there anything in your life you wish you'd done differently?

185

I wish I'd studied harder. And met my wife earlier.

. . .

I first found out I had cancer on March 21 of this year. I went into the hospital and they x-rayed me, and the next day they operated for cancer. I never dreamt of ever having it—I never had any real symptoms. They took the x-ray, and they operated on me immediately. They said they didn't get it all.

But since I've been here at the hospice, I've improved one hundred percent from what I was. I'm pain-free, and I look like I might live forever. I don't know how long I've got, but they've got me stabilized so that I can live a decent life on a daily basis. This is a great place. The most wonderful place I've ever been in. . . . They're the very best. Everyone from the ones that clean the rugs right up to the top are just as nice as they can be. They're all friendly, and they're all willing to do for you—to make you comfortable.

*Did your attitude towards life change after you
learned that you have cancer?*

Well, it changes your life—you don't know what to do at first. It brought my family closer together. We never were astray, but when I got sick, they all got together to help me.

My children and grandchildren all live in the area. . . . So some or all of them show up during the week.

*Do you have any advice for other people about how
they should live their lives?*

You should live your life, and live it to the fullest while you can. And take care of your health while you're doing it. That's the most important thing. We smoke too much, and drink too much, and don't get enough rest. And of course we eat too much bad food. I'm not a food faddist, and I believe that if you want a hot dog or hamburger, you can have it, but you don't make a steady diet of it.

I don't believe there's any set rule. Everybody has to play the game the way they see it. And they usually don't accept too much advice from anybody anyway.

How did you feel when the doctors told you that you might not have much time left?

Well, it didn't shake me up as much as I thought it would. I couldn't believe it at first—I think it was too much to swallow. And then as time went on, I'd be laying in bed and get to thinking about it, and then I'd cry. When I realized how important it is. I just can't believe that my life is set short.

ॐ

TOM WIEGAND
HOSPICE OF ST. JOSEPH COUNTY

I have five brothers and sisters. I've always lived in the South Bend [Indiana] area. For the first five years of my life, I lived out in the country. I have a form of muscular dystrophy. I had two brothers who were twins who also had it. Both have passed away. For most of my life, I've lived in a wheelchair. In the country, the closest home was a quarter of a mile away. It was fairly isolated, so I read a great deal of my life.

. . .

I started out with homebound education. In homebound education, a teacher comes to the home after or before school hours and provides a couple hours of schooling. When I started my second year of school, I was sent to a special education program in South Bend. . . . At that time, I did five years of school in three years. I've always loved to read, and I've always loved to learn, so I flew through that. But when I started the fifth grade, I was transferred back to homebound education because the school was closed. And from the sixth until the time the state was no longer obligated to provide anything, I had homebound education. When I started high school, because of Indiana law at the time, I could only get two classes per semester. So obviously there was no chance to get a diploma. And at eighteen, when the state didn't do any more, I gave up, and didn't do anything for a while.

And then about four or five years later, as the disability rights movement started, I got involved with an organization called the Spinal Cord Injury Foundation, and decided to go back and get my GED. I went to school at Indiana University at South Bend.

At about the same time, I got very intensely involved with the Spinal Cord Injury Foundation, and for the next five years I served as the President of that organization, and was really involved in disability rights. . . .

After about five years of that, I got really burned out, so I went into business with another guy who was disabled, and we sold wheelchairs and other medical equipment. After about two years of that, it was apparent I'd made a mistake. I was killing my body, because I'd be up at 6:30, get into work at 9:30 or 10:00, work until 5:00 or 6:00 in the evening, and then come home and go to bed. Two years of that was about all I could take, so I sold the business and got married. Which I never expected to do. It surprised a lot of people, believe me. We just celebrated our tenth anniversary.

The strangest thing in my whole life was the day of the marriage. We had an evening service, and I was in a little room behind the altar, waiting for the music. My best friend, who was a woman, was standing up with me. We heard the music and came out. There were about 150 of our family and friends who had made it real clear they wanted to be there when they heard we were getting married. We were just going to have immediate family, but they wouldn't tolerate that. And when we came out, they were all crying. Just for a brief instant, I thought, "Is this a funeral or a wedding?"

I've had a lot of support from a lot of nice people. They were just very happy that it had worked out for us.

I met my wife because she had gotten a ticket for parking in a handicapped parking spot. [Mr. Wiegand's wife is also in a wheelchair.] It was before she knew there was such a thing as handicapped parking license plates. The judge didn't make her pay a fine, but he told her she had to get information, so she came to the organization that I was the head of. And after about three years of talking to each other and working together on different projects—she was in an unhappy marriage which she ended—one day she called me up and told me she loved me, was I interested? I thought, "Hell yes, I am!"

. . .

I guess I had never thought that I would be married. It proved to be the smartest thing I ever did.

. . .

I got involved with the Spinal Cord Injury Foundation because the person who was the head of it at the time was an FBI agent in the South Bend area who was married to a disabled woman. As part of his job, he was doing a background check on one of our neighbors. . . . When he came to the house to talk to us to see if we had anything to say about these people, he left a newsletter that the organization produced. After reading it, I decided I'd like to go to a meeting, so that's what I did. I met a lot of interesting people, started reading what was going on at the national level, and just got really involved in it.

. . .

189

When my sister joined the Navy and went to Jacksonville, my parents and I went to visit her. And in traveling around the next five or ten years, I saw how a lot of different people lived, and also found out how rare I was. It was quite evident that a lot of restaurants had never had to deal with someone in a wheelchair. And all the cliches you ever heard about—waitresses talking to someone else rather than me—all of those things, we dealt with. It was real easy to make the jump to try to change things, because it wasn't a good feeling.

[When I was growing up], because of my personality, I was always comfortable reading or watching tv, so I never really got involved with thinking about what my future would be, because I didn't expect to have one. When I was about nine years old, I participated in a muscular dystrophy program, and at the end of that process, the doctors said that I wouldn't live to be thirteen. I guess I kind of accepted that, rather than fight it. So we all kind of accepted that that's what would happen. Now here I am at forty-seven, and it hasn't happened yet. Although sometimes I wish it would. . . .

I think Dr. Kevorkian has some good ideas. As this [disease] progresses, and I lose more and more, it becomes clearer what the end of my life is going to be like. I'd probably opt for assisted suicide. . . . We won't do anything about it, because it's too dangerous for [my wife]. But if it were possible, I might do that.

What would be the point at which you'd want to do that?

I think after I lose all my mobility. I'm so used to being able to go out every day. My wife had decided to go back and get her GED and go to college. A couple years ago, she started pursuing a Ph.D. in psychology. She'll be a sixty year old psychologist. Her professors tell her it will be great, because the baby boomers will need peers to help them. So I go into school with her. I like hanging out over at the university, in the library, talking with people there. And when I have to give that up, most of the quality will go out of my life.

. . .

What are the things that have made you the happiest?

Being married—it's harder than I thought and better than I ever thought. Some of my friends. My best friend, I've known since she was sixteen and I was twenty. My nieces and nephews. And I just became a grandfather this weekend. My stepdaughter had a baby boy. They named him Robert Thomas, which made me feel nice. . . . They really wanted to have a baby who they could name after me before I died, because I have a really good relationship with my step-daughter.

Does that make you feel old?

Incredibly. I used to babysit my niece—my sister's girl—when she was in kindergarten. We had a really good relation-ship—I've been especially close to all my nieces and nephews. Now she is also expecting in August, and that makes me feel incredibly old, because I remember really well taking care of her. I guess it's one of the things that the dying process makes clearer—that time does pass and there is a change of genera-tions, an ongoing process.

Is that a good kind of feeling?

Yeah, it's nice to know that there will be parts of me that go on. At the same time, it makes me angry, because I would very much like to live another five hundred years. I'd take five hundred years. I've always been fascinated by history, and the way things change—all of that. I would very much like to know what's going to happen in the future.

191

Do you think there's any particular meaning or purpose to life?

Yeah, I think there is a purpose. I'm not sure what it is. I can't believe in coincidence because, if it's coincidental, I've had some incredible things happen, like meeting my wife. I think there is a purpose. I wish it were clearer what it is. But I guess that's one of the things that makes dying not too bad, because I think that we will know after we die. . . .

I hope there's a life after death. I don't know. I'm not a strongly religious person, but I hope there is something.

Is there anything in your life that you wish you'd done differently?

Yeah, I wish I'd known when I was in my twenties what I know now about how we could have been more aggressive, more demanding of our rights, and worked harder to change things.

Do you have any advice for other people about how they should live their lives?

Yeah—live today. So many people I know live in the past or waste the day worrying about the future. They don't see what's going on today. They don't appreciate sitting and watching birds. We have a squirrel feeder on our front porch, and have three or four different squirrels go up every day. Appreciating what goes on with nature, and things like that. Taking the time to tell someone that they look nice, or that you love them. People just don't live today. They spend all their time worrying about tomorrow or the past. They can't do anything about either one.

That's something that has become clearer to me lately. The sense of time passing increases the pressure of there not being enough time to do everything I want to do. Not enough time to see this little grandbaby grow up. The stronger that pressure, that feeling of time flying away, makes it really in focus that people spend so much time being dishonest, not telling people how they really feel. Worrying about what happened in the past. They don't take the time to help other people, and care for other people. Or to care for themselves. And they don't seem to realize that time goes by really fast.

Appendix

Hospice Descriptions

HOSPICE DESCRIPTIONS

This book is not about hospices. Accordingly, I included the interviewees' comments about hospices only when I felt such comments related to the subjects that are the focus of this book. I would like to emphasize, however, that virtually everyone I interviewed had nothing but the highest praise for his or her hospice, the services the hospice provided, and the people who provided them. As one interviewee said:

> I've never met such a group of people—from top to bottom. They are always caring. They're never pushy. They never try to press their point of view. They're always supportive and caring. That's all they are. They're not in it for anything else. . . . No matter what the crisis is, they're there supporting you. They never are judgmental. They never talk about our lifestyle or anything like that. They're just there, to try to make my death easier.

In working on this book, my experience with hospices has also been extremely positive. The people with whom I have dealt have been uniformly friendly, helpful, and supportive. I am convinced, based on my personal experiences and my conversations with hospice patients, that hospices provide an extremely valuable service to people in very difficult circumstances, and that they do so with extraordinary skill, dedication, and compassion.

The following are descriptions of the hospices whose patients were interviewed for this book. These descriptions were prepared in 1994.

ALLEGHENY HOSPICE

Allegheny Hospice is located in Pittsburgh, Pennsylvania. The hospice has offered services since 1979 as a hospital-based agency affiliated with Allegheny General Hospital. The hospice helps approximately two hundred patients/families annually. The hospice's focus of care is the provision of comfort, rather than a cure. The hospice works with families to maintain patients in their homes, control pain, and improve the quality of life by addressing social, emotional, and spiritual needs.

Patients receive services from team members who provide care in patients' homes. The team includes nurses, home health aides, social workers, clergy, and a core of volunteers. The hospice also offers bereavement support for family members. These services include bereavement counseling, support groups, memorial services, and special family celebrations.

The hospice offers a program called Celebrations of a Lifetime, which is a cooperative effort of Allegheny Hospice, Allegheny General Hospital, and the Western Chapter Pennsylvania Restaurant Association. This program enhances special occasions such as birthdays and anniversaries for terminally ill patients.

The hospice gives patients and their families the opportunity to make choices regarding their care. It helps create an environment that allows them to live each day to its fullest, in a peaceful and dignified manner.

ANGELA HOSPICE

Angela Hospice is located in Livonia, Michigan, near Detroit. In 1974, Sister Mary Giovanni Monge attended a seminar in England given by Dr. Cicely Saunders and decided that southeast Michigan was sorely lacking in services to care for people suffering from incurable illnesses, and the families of such people, without taxing the monetary resources of either the individual or the institutions providing health care insurance. After eleven years of research and preparation, Sister Giovanni, under the sponsorship of the Felician Sisters of the Presentation Province, founded Angela Hospice Home Care, Inc., in 1985.

In 1991, construction began on the Angela Hospice Care Center, located on the Felician Sisters' grounds in Livonia. The facility contains a patient day-care center, where primary caregivers may bring their loved ones for the day so they can continue to work, run errands, or receive much-needed respite. The center also contains rooms with a homelike environment for patients, private family rooms, a volunteer training room, a family lounge chapel, a children's room, physicians' offices, a nurses' station, and administrative offices, among others. The staff provides physical, emotional, and spiritual support twenty-four hours a day.

ARBOR HOSPICE

Arbor Hospice is a not-for-profit, nondenominational, community-based organization that has served greater southeastern Michigan since 1984. It has offices in Ann Arbor and Allen Park, Michigan. The hospice is a member of the National Hospice Organization, Hospice Association of America, National Association of Home Care, Michigan Hospice Organization, and Michigan Association of Home Care.

The hospice provides a comprehensive set of services designed to address the physical, emotional, and spiritual needs of individuals and families who face life-threatening illnesses. Hospice care is supervised by the patient's own physician or one of the hospice's staff medical directors. Care is provided by a team of professionals, including registered nurses, home health aides, social workers, therapists, bereavement staff, clergy, volunteers, and others who have specific areas of expertise and can address the various needs of patient, family, and other caregivers during the illness. The hospice strives to create an environment in which its patients can achieve the highest quality of life possible, within the limitations of their illnesses.

CABRINI HOSPICE

Cabrini Hospice, located in New York City, provides a program of care and support designed to meet the special needs of patients in advanced stages of illnesses, as well as their families and significant friends. Cabrini's hospice program was founded in 1980 by Father Vincent Pulicano, who was at that time the director of pastoral care at Cabrini Medical Center. Through his own personal struggle with cancer, Father Vincent learned first-hand of the need to provide highly personalized palliative and supportive care. Father Vincent lived to see his dream come true; Cabrini Hospice opened in October 1980, four months before his death.

The hospice offers a coordinated program of home-care services for persons living with advanced illnesses. The hospice team develops a program of care for each individual, and the necessary medical and support services are delivered to patients within the home. The hospice also has an inpatient unit specially designed to foster a comfortable, homelike atmosphere; it is available for patients when short-term acute hospital care is necessary.

The hospice's goals are to promote optimum comfort and a personal sense of control, with the focus on quality of life. The hospice also offers the opportunity for personal and spiritual healing. Cabrini views hospice as being about living life fully and using all the options available. Patients are encouraged to set whatever goals are right for them and to maintain beliefs that provide direction and support.

CLOVER HOSPICE

Clover Hospice, located in Auburn, Maine, opened in May 1982. The hospice is an inpatient facility that provides care for terminally ill individuals who have a prognosis of six or fewer months to live. The hospice has focused from the start on acknowledging the eventuality of death and helping terminally ill patients and their families deal with it in a forthright, honest manner. The hospice's goal is to facilitate death with dignity; freedom from pain is the primary means to that end.

The hospice is a place where patients' mental, emotional, and spiritual needs are addressed, as well as their medical and physical needs. Families are encouraged to share in the care of their loved ones to the extent they feel comfortable. The hospice also provides overnight accommodations. The patients' surroundings are made as homelike as possible, thus sparing them the stresses and fears that may be associated with more traditional hospital settings.

FAMILY HOME HOSPICE

Family Home Hospice was activated in Las Vegas, Nevada, in October 1989 to serve as the preferred provider of hospice support for the members of Health Plan of Nevada, a HMO, or who are otherwise insured by Sierra Health Services, as well as by Medicare and all other insurance products. The hospice has grown at a slow, planned rate to its present status as the second-largest hospice in Nevada. It is a member of the National Hospice Organization and adheres to the standards of that body. It is also licensed as a home health care agency by the state of Nevada.

The hospice focuses on assisting caregivers in maintaining the patient at home, in comfort, free of pain, and with the best quality of life possible. When continued home care is impossible, the hospice assists family and caregivers to place the patient in a proper setting, which may include nursing homes in the service area. The hospice provides a full range of services through a full-time staff of professionals, augmented by hospice volunteers and contract providers as needed for special situations. One of the hospice team's goals is to have the patient and family participate to the maximum extent possible in planning for and providing the care. Family Home Hospice also offers a complete bereavement support service, at no cost, to the community at large.

HEART OF AMERICA HOSPICE

Heart of America Hospice, located in Kansas City, Missouri, was formed in the spring of 1993 to provide traditional hospice care in patients' homes, as well as a specialized focus on those whose homes are in long-term care facilities. It is licensed in Kansas and Missouri and is Medicare and Medicaid certified.

Hospice is a concept of care that provides services for patients who are diagnosed as having life-limiting illnesses. Each patient and family is addressed as the care unit. Comprehensive and loving support is given through the interdisciplinary team, which consists of physicians, nurses, home health aides, social workers, chaplains, and counselors. The hospice's holistic approach considers not only physical but also emotional, spiritual, and social needs of patient and family. Pain control and symptom management are keys to patient comfort. The hospice seeks to provide the highest quality of life possible, promote the dignity of the life process, and provide assistance in the final days of the patient's journey.

HOSPICE CARE OF THE
VISITING NURSE ASSOCIATION

Hospice Care of the Visiting Nurse Association is a charitable, nonprofit hospice agency that provides complete hospice care services for patients and families facing life-limiting illnesses in the Kansas City area. The hospice's services are available to all residents of the ten-county metropolitan area regardless of age, race, sex, color, religion, or national origin. The hospice's focus is on quality of life, providing emotional support for patients and their families, pain and symptom management, and helping make the individual's remaining time as special as possible.

The hospice develops a plan of care based on the unique needs of the patient and family. The care team may consist of the patient's primary physician, nurses, home health aides, social workers, chaplains, and volunteers. The care team members are specially trained to work with families facing terminal illnesses and are available to make home visits—scheduled and unscheduled—twenty-four hours a day, seven days a week. The hospice also offers grief recovery services to provide support to family members and friends.

HOSPICE OF OKLAHOMA COUNTY

The Hospice of Oklahoma County is located in Oklahoma City. It is a Medicare certified, nonprofit agency dedicated to providing physical, emotional, and spiritual care for the terminally ill and their families. It was founded in 1990 by physicians of the Oklahoma County Medical Society.

The Hospice of Oklahoma County is a member of the National Hospice Organization and subscribes to its standards. It is also licensed in Oklahoma and is a member of the Oklahoma State Hospital Organization.

The hospice's focus is on providing care at home. When that does not seem possible, the primary physician and the hospice team make arrangements for hospital or nursing home admission, with continuity of care. When the team identifies problems beyond its expertise (legal, financial, etc.), it refers the family to other community resources.

The hospice develops an individual plan of care. Each patient/family may choose the services they wish to receive. On-call help is available twenty-four hours a day, seven days a week.

HOSPICE OF ST. JOSEPH COUNTY, INC.

The Hospice of St. Joseph County, Inc., is located in South Bend, Indiana. It was incorporated in 1978 and served its first patient in 1980. The hospice's policy is to attempt to dignify, help prepare for, and make a positive experience of the patient's dying.

The hospice care program provides many additional facets in the care of the patient and his or her family. It includes not only physical care of the patient and supervision of medication under the direction of the attending physician, but also spiritual counseling when appropriate, social work services, home health aide assistance, volunteers, counseling, emotional support, and a bereavement program for survivors. This combination of services allows patients to stay in their homes, with their families or caregivers, during their terminal illnesses.

HOSPICE SAN ANTONIO

Hospice San Antonio was founded in 1983 and is the oldest hospice program in San Antonio and Bexar County. Hospice San Antonio is a not-for-profit organization, directed by a board of directors representing the community. It is part of the United Way of San Antonio and Bexar County. The hospice is state licensed and a member of the National Hospice Organization and the Texas Hospice Organization.

Hospice San Antonio helps terminally ill patients and their families maintain personal dignity and enhance the quality of life as they cope with the dying process. When curative treatment is no longer possible or desired, the hospice offers medical care in a life-affirming atmosphere as an alternative to hospitalization. The patient is encouraged to maintain control over decisions and prepare for death in his or her own way. The hospice's primary goals are pain relief and symptom management. Family members and caregivers also receive support, guidance, and reassurance. This care continues during the bereavement period.

McKENZIE-WILLAMETTE HOSPICE

McKenzie-Willamette Hospice was founded in Springfield, Oregon, in 1984. It was one of the first agencies in Oregon to become Medicare certified. The hospice serves a varied community in the Springfield/Eugene area. Located in Southern Willamette Valley, it serves both a small urban and a rural population. The hospice's mission is to increase access to and availability of hospice services to the community, particularly to people in nursing homes, foster homes, and other alternative settings.

In the last few years, the hospice has experienced rapid growth due to its flexibility and its examination of the community's needs. The hospice program has broadened its care, not only to utilize the traditional aspects of hospice—such as nursing, social work, volunteers, and home health aides—but

205

also to include day care for caregiver respite and massage therapy for pain and symptom control.

MOUNTAIN AREA HOSPICE

Mountain Area Hospice is located in Asheville, North Carolina. It was established in 1978 and serves all of Buscombe County, the largest county in North Carolina. The hospice is primarily a home-based program; it cared for more than four hundred patients in 1993. It enables patients to live at home, amid familiar surroundings, with friends and loved ones, for as long as possible. The hospice also has an inpatient facility, called Solace, for individuals who cannot live at home.

The hospice program seeks to allow persons with end-stage terminal illnesses to live in dignity and serenity, as free as possible of pain and other distressing symptoms. The services the hospice provides include pain and other symptom management, spiritual counseling, family counseling, and bereavement services. The hospice program recognizes the emotional and physical strains that caring for a person with advanced disease usually places on family members. The program seeks to ease emotional and physical problems, provide spiritual assistance, and give supportive care to those bearing that burden. The patients and their family systems are the focus of hospice care.

ST. VINCENT HOSPICE

St. Vincent Hospice is located in Indianapolis, Indiana. It provides a special way of caring for the person whose life expectancy is limited. The hospice affirms life and maintains the dignity of each individual it serves. The program focuses on maintaining the quality of life by controlling the patient's symptoms and keeping him or her comfortable, while providing for spiritual, emotional, social, and physical needs. The hospice is a concept of care, not a place of care. It focuses on caring for patients in the familiar settings of their own homes whenever possible. However, the hospice also has an inpatient unit and other multiple inpatient sites that are medically directed by the attending hospice physician and that provide hospice nursing care seven days a week, twenty-four hours a day.

The hospice team—including physicians, nurses, social workers, clergy, and highly trained volunteers—works together with the physician, patient, and family to develop a treatment plan. Social service team members are available to help ease family tensions and support family members in their grief. Chaplain services also are available, but freedom of religious belief or nonbelief is respected. In addition, the hospice provides bereavement support to help family and friends cope with grief and loss for at least thirteen months following the death.

VNA HOSPICE

VNA Hospice is an agency of the Visiting Nurse Association of Cleveland. The hospice offers a specialized health care program that emphasizes the management of pain and other symptoms usually associated with terminal illness. The hospice offers patient- and family-centered care. Care is provided by a hospice interdisciplinary team of specially trained medical professionals and lay persons. The hospice can also enhance the care given to facility residents with terminal illnesses by providing supplemental personnel and services, personal care, feeding, companionship, family counseling, and techniques for controlling pain.

The hospice is committed to the belief that the hospice concept of care reaffirms the right of every person and family to participate fully in the final stage of life. The hospice concept recognizes dying as a normal process and neither hastens nor postpones death. The hospice believes that, with appropriate care and support, the person in the last stage of life can live fully and with dignity, free of pain and other discomforts.

ORDER FORM

ORDERS BY PHONE and **ORDERING INFORMATION:**
CALL 1(800)247-6553

To order copies of LOOKING BACK by phone, or for information regarding orders, call BookMasters toll free at 1(800)247-6553. Payment may be made by credit card (AMEX, Discover, MasterCard or VISA accepted), check or money order. The price for a single copy is $11.95, plus $2.50 for shipping and handling, for a total of $14.45.* (Sales tax will be added to books shipped to New York or Ohio addresses. For the amount of tax, please call the toll free number listed above.) For prices for multiple copies, or for information regarding orders by fax, please call BookMasters at the number listed above.

ORDERS BY MAIL

To order copies of LOOKING BACK by mail, fill out the form below and mail to the following address, together with check or money order (please do not send cash):

> BookMasters, Inc.
> P.O. Box 2039
> Mansfield, OH   44905

Please send me _____ copies of LOOKING BACK. I have enclosed a check/money order in the amount of $_____. (For prices, including sales tax for orders shipped to New York or Ohio addresses, see instructions above in section regarding orders by phone, or call 1(800)247-6553.)

Name: _____

Address: _____

City: _____   State: _____

Zip Code: _____

Phone: (_____) _____

LOOKING BACK is also listed on the World Wide Web at: http://www.bookmasters.com/elecmkt.htm

* Orders are generally mailed within 48 hours. Orders are sent book rate. For expedited delivery, shipping and handling costs will be higher. Call BookMasters for further information.

CALL *TOLL FREE* AND ORDER NOW!